EASY
ONE-DISH
DINNER
RECIPES

T0001556

© 2023 Fox Chapel Publishing Company, Inc., 903 Square Street, Mount Joy, PA 17552.

ISBN 978-1-4971-0387-0

Recipe selection, design, and book design © Fox Chapel Publishing. Recipes and photographs © G&R Publishing DBA CQ Products, unless otherwise noted.

The following images are from Shutterstock.com: background texture on back jacket and throughout interior: StevanZZ; back jacket top, 4–5 background: Netrun78; 7, 64: Brent Hofacker; 8 top: stockphotofan1; 8 middle: Volodymyr Nik; 11 top: SrideeStudio; 11 bottom: lyly; 13: Ground Picture; 34: Gabrielle Hovey; 36: etorres; 63: El Nariz; 87: Africa Studio; 136: Elena Shashkina; 138–139: Leigh Anne Meeks

Library of Congress Control Number: 2023937417

To learn more about the other great books from Fox Chapel Publishing, or to find a retailer near you, call toll-free 800-457-9112 or visit us at www.FoxChapelPublishing.com.

We are always looking for talented authors. To submit an idea, please send a brief inquiry to acquisitions@foxchapelpublishing.com.

Printed in China
First printing

EASY
ONE-DISH
DINNER
RECIPES

Delicious, Time-Saving Meals to Make in Just One Pot, Sheet Pan, Skillet, Dutch Oven, and More

By Gabrielle Garcia

FOX CHAPEL
PUBLISHING

Contents

22

35

53

60

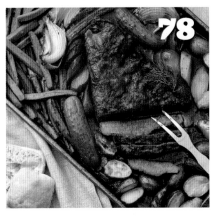
78

89

109

119

Welcome to Stress-Free Cooking!

One-dish meals not only save you from a massive clean-up, but they also save you time spent multitasking. Whether you're cooking for yourself or your family, you want a filling or a light meal, or you just want to try a fun new recipe, this book has what you're looking for. "One-dish" refers to the cooking method used: some of the recipes call for single baking sheets while others call for skillets, and a few even recommend firing up the grill. In any case, cleanup will be a breeze.

What you'll need:

- **Baking sheets** (sheet pans) are used for many of these recipes.
- **Skillets, saucepans, and cast-iron skillets** are essential to many of the one-dish recipes! Some also require a covering method, whether that be a lid or aluminum foil.
- **Pizza pans** are needed for a few of the pizza recipes. If you don't have one, use a baking sheet instead.
- **A grill** is recommended for some of the recipes, like kebabs and foil packs. Cooking kebabs or foil packs in the oven is a great alternative if you don't want to fire up the grill. Many of these recipes also require metal or wooden skewers or heavy-duty foil.
- **Muffin pans** are suggested in some cases, but you can always use a baking sheet instead.
- **Mason jars** are used in a few quick salad recipes.
- **Mugs** are used in a few recipes, sometimes for serving and sometimes for meal preparation.
- At least one recipe requires a **loaf pan**.

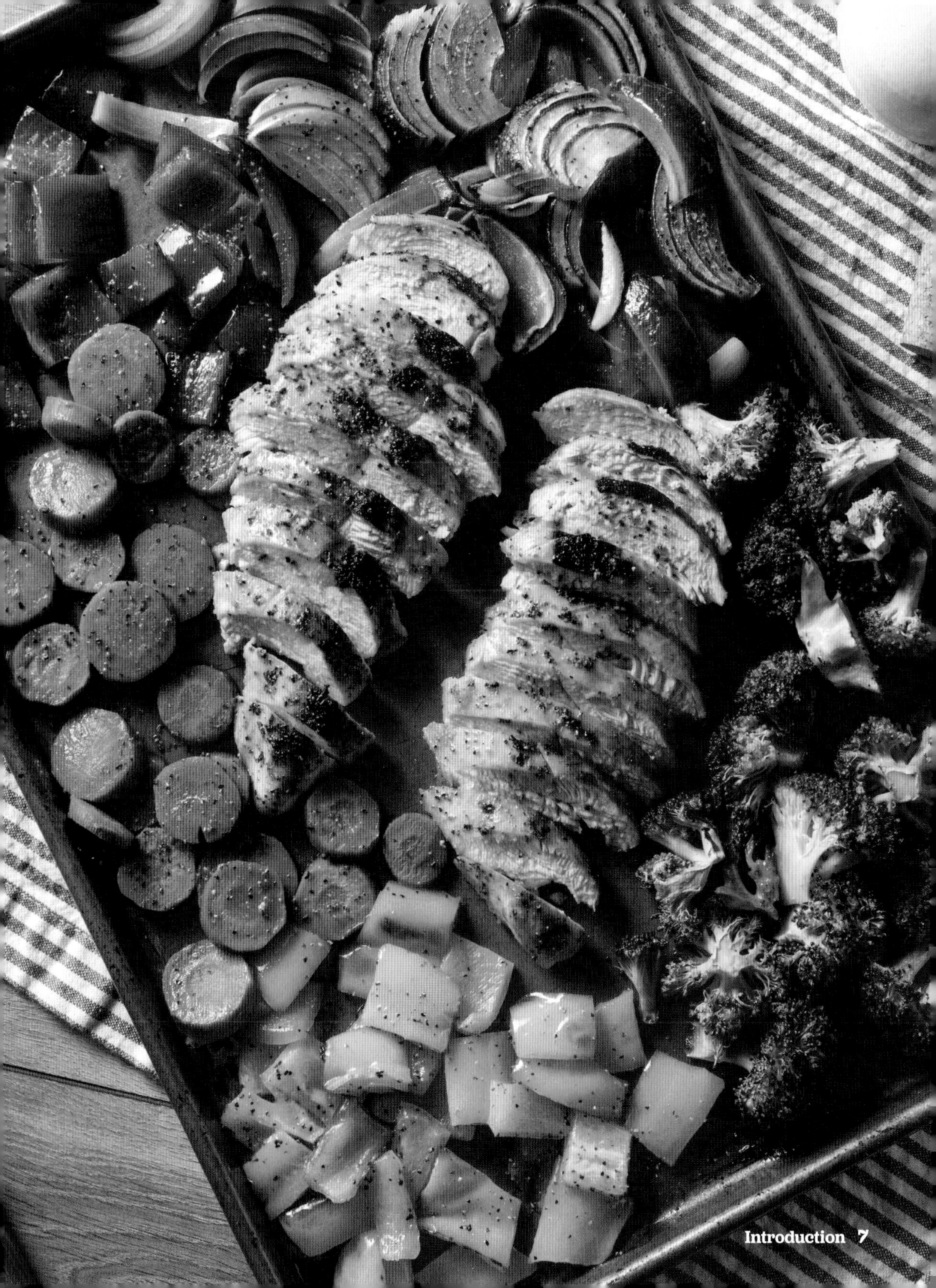

Baking Sheet Preparation and Care

It's necessary to grease or line your baking sheet. You can grease your pan with cooking spray, butter, or any cooking oil you have handy. When it comes to greasing, you don't want to use too much or too little, and you need to cover the entire surface, including the sides. For less cleanup, line your pan with foil, parchment paper, or a nonstick silicone baking mat. For the crispiest result, grease your baking sheet and bake directly on the bare sheet. For the most evenly roasted finish and a less charred appearance, line your sheet with parchment paper. For results in the middle, choose foil or a nonstick silicone baking mat. Whatever you choose, your finished product will be filled with flavor!

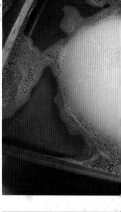

When it comes to cleaning your baking sheet, a simple sponge and soap will be quickest, but may not be the most thorough. To make sure your baking sheet doesn't build up grime over time, it's important to occasionally take some extra time to scrub it clean. There are a few different methods you can use to deep-clean your pan:

- **Baking soda and vinegar—** Mix equal amounts of baking soda and white distilled vinegar to create a paste. Spread the paste across the entire sheet pan and let sit for at least 30 minutes. Scrub the pan with a damp, rough sponge, then rinse it with warm soapy water. Depending on how dirty your pan is, this method can take more time and require extra scrubbing.

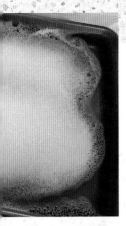

- **Oven cleaning spray (such as Easy-Off®) and a steel wool scrub pad**—First, spray the pan's surface with the oven cleaning spray (be wary of the strong scent) and place it into the oven, letting it sit for 20 minutes. Then put the baking sheet into the sink and run warm water over top, scrubbing the surface with the steel wool scrub pad. After the surface appears fully scrubbed, wash the pan with warm, soapy water.

- **Baking soda and hydrogen peroxide**—This final method requires a longer soaking time but less scrubbing. You will need baking soda, hydrogen peroxide topical solution, a plastic scraper, and a scrubbing sponge. Sprinkle the baking soda across the surface of the pan, almost blanketing it. Spray a generous amount of the hydrogen peroxide over the baking soda until it is wet. Let the pan sit overnight (for at least 8 hours). When finished, scrape the baking soda and peroxide mixture into the trash, then rinse your pan and wash it in warm, soapy water with the scrubbing sponge.

Keep in mind that in most cases, especially if you line your pan, it won't require deep-cleaning. No matter what, always soak your pan with soapy water and clean it with a sponge after each use to ensure less grime build-up over time. Always dry immediately to prevent potential rusting. And remember, it's rare to have a pan without blotches, stains, and wear!

When greasing your pan, be sure to completely cover the surfaces, including the bottom and up the sides.

Skillet and Saucepan Care

Make sure your skillet is oven-safe and has a lid. If it does not have a lid, use foil to cover your skillet when needed. You will need a medium to large skillet or saucepan for most of the recipes in this book. For saucepan cleanup, some simple soap and warm water will do, and you may occasionally need to soak the pan if it's extra grimy. However, cast-iron skillets need more tender loving care to maintain their cooking abilities.

Seasoning Cast Iron

Seasoning is vital not only for coating the cookware to prevent rust, but also for creating a natural, permanent, nonstick cooking surface. Start by preparing your oven: put foil on the bottom to catch any drips and set it to 350°F. Then rub a thin layer of vegetable oil or shortening over all the surfaces of your cast-iron skillet and set the pan upside down on the oven rack for 1 hour. Turn off the oven and let the pan cool completely; then wipe with a paper towel. Refresh as needed and cook periodically with oil to build patina.

Seasoning is a must for cast-iron skillets. Use vegetable oil or shortening for the best results.

Cleaning Cast Iron

It's best to avoid using dish soap when cleaning cast iron, since it strips off the seasoning, but if you feel it's necessary, use it sparingly and remember to refresh the seasoning on your cookware afterward. Regular cleaning maintenance can be done with or without water:

You can clean cast iron with or without water to preserve the seasoning and preservation of the cookware.

With water: Use very hot water and a stiff nylon brush or scrubber (soap strips off the seasoning and can seep into the metal). Rinse and wipe the pan dry with paper towels or an old towel (cast iron can leave black stains). Then set the pan on a burner over low heat to remove any remaining moisture and prevent rust.

Without water: Scrub the pan with coarse salt or a plastic scraper and wipe it with a clean rag.

Storing Cast Iron

After all the moisture has been removed and your pan is cool, store it uncovered in a dry location. Remember not to reseason your cookware before you store it, or the oil could turn rancid before you use it again. If rust appears, scrub it off with steel wool and reseason.

Store your cleaned and dry cast-iron cookware in a dry location.

Managing Your Time

While all these recipes are timesaving and nearly mess-free, planning your mealtimes and preparation will help you stay even more organized and stress-free in the kitchen. None of these recipes require preparations the night before, but planning ahead will help if you want to save extra time the night of your meal. Try some of the following tips:

- Cut up vegetables and fruit ahead of time and keep them in storage containers or bags until you're ready to cook. You can also buy frozen or pre-cut fruit and vegetables, including lettuce, to save even more time!

- For rice recipes, buy quick-cooking rice in ready-to-go packets.

- For burgers, opt for pre-made patties that can go straight to the grill or stovetop.

- Take marinades into consideration when planning your meal. Marinades should sit at least 30 minutes to an hour for the best flavor. You can easily marinate something overnight if you want to start cooking your meat right away the night of.

- Use the recipes in the Shortcut Sides section starting on page 128 to quickly add healthy, tasty accents to any meal!

Food Safety

It's extremely important when cooking eggs or meat of any kind to check the temperature to ensure your food is thoroughly cooked. It is best to use a good meat thermometer to prevent under- or over-cooking. The USDA recommends the following minimum internal temperatures:

- Fish: 145°F
- Beef Roasts: 145°F (rare) to 160°F (medium) to 170°F (well done)
- Ground Beef: 160°F
- Ground Poultry: 165°F
- Chicken Breasts: 170°F
- Whole Poultry and Parts (thighs, wings): 180°F
- Pork (chops, tenderloins): 160°F
- Ground Pork: 160°F
- Egg Dishes: 160°F
- Reheated Foods: 165°F or until hot and steaming

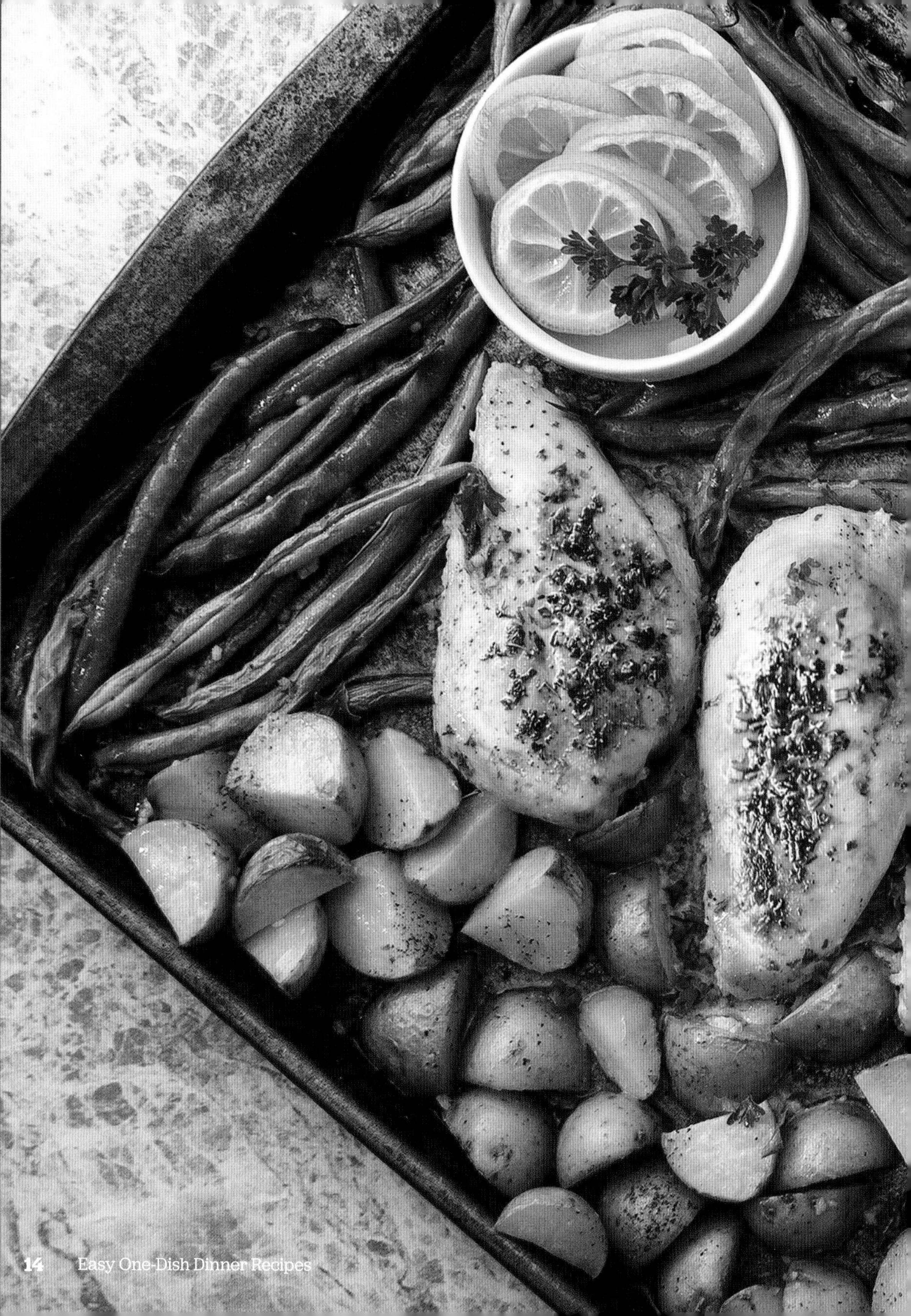

Quick Chicken & Turkey

One of the easiest starting points for a quick, healthy meal is poultry! Chicken and turkey are great lean proteins you can easily season and adapt to suit any type of cuisine. From classic pot pies to modern fusion wraps, humble poultry is the perfect base for family-friendly meals, dinner party mains, and date night delights.

Asiago Turkey & Roasted Caesar

Serves 3

Ingredients

- » **1 head cauliflower**
- » **Olive oil**
- » **Salt and black pepper to taste**
- » **1 garlic bulb**
- » **Three 6- to 7-ounce turkey breast cutlets**
- » **⅓ cup grated Asiago cheese, plus more for serving**
- » **⅓ cup panko breadcrumbs**
- » **1 tablespoon chopped fresh parsley**
- » **1 romaine heart**
- » **Anchovy paste to taste**
- » **Worcestershire sauce to taste**
- » **Lemon wedges for serving**

1. Preheat the oven to 450°F and grease or line your sheet pan. Cut the cauliflower into florets and dump onto the prepped pan; drizzle with 2 tablespoons of oil, toss to coat, arrange in a single layer, and sprinkle with salt and black pepper.

2. Remove the papery skin from the garlic bulb and cut off the top ¼", exposing the individual cloves. Set the garlic on a piece of foil large enough to wrap around the bulb; drizzle the cloves with oil, wrap the foil around the bulb, and set the bundle on the pan with the cauliflower. Bake for 30 minutes, stirring the cauliflower once or twice.

3. Drizzle a little oil over the cauliflower if it seems dry and move the florets to one side of the pan. Season the turkey cutlets with salt and black pepper and arrange in the center of the pan.

4. In a bowl, combine the cheese, breadcrumbs, parsley, 1½ tablespoons of oil, and a little salt and black pepper. Divide the mixture among the turkey cutlets and press gently to adhere; bake for 10 minutes, until the crumbs are golden.

5. Cut the romaine heart lengthwise into three wedges and arrange them on the open side of the pan; drizzle with 1 tablespoon of oil and season with salt and black pepper. Bake 5 minutes, until the turkey is cooked through (165°F), the cauliflower is tender, and the romaine has browned at the edges.

6. Spread some of the roasted garlic from the cloves over the food as desired, refrigerating any remaining garlic for use in another recipe. Spread anchovy paste over the romaine and drizzle with Worcestershire sauce. Squeeze the juice from the lemon wedges over everything. Serve with Asiago for sprinkling.

Honey-Pineapple Chicken Fajitas

Ingredients

- » **2 tablespoons coconut oil, melted**
- » **1 tablespoon chili powder**
- » **2 teaspoons ground cumin**
- » **1 teaspoon garlic powder**
- » **1½ teaspoons salt**
- » **2 tablespoons honey**
- » **2 tablespoons lime juice**
- » **1½ pounds boneless, skinless chicken breasts, cut into bite-size pieces**
- » **1 sweet onion, sliced into half-moons**
- » **2 red bell peppers, cut into strips**
- » **2 green bell peppers, cut into strips**
- » **One 20-ounce can pineapple chunks, drained**
- » **Twelve 6" corn or flour tortillas**
- » **Pico de gallo, sour cream, sliced jalapeño peppers, sliced avocado, and lime wedges for serving**

1. Preheat the oven to 425°F and grease or line your sheet pan. In a big bowl, whisk together the oil, chili powder, cumin, garlic powder, salt, honey, and lime juice. Add the chicken, onion, bell peppers, and pineapple and toss to coat. Dump the mixture onto the prepared pan in a single layer. Bake for 20 minutes.

2. Remove the pan from the oven and preheat your broiler. Broil for a few minutes, until the vegetables have lightly browned, and the chicken is no longer pink.

3. Warm the tortillas, fill them with chicken and vegetables, and top them with pico de gallo, sour cream, jalapeño peppers, and avocado; squeeze juice from the lime wedges over the food.

Serves
6

Cuban Cha-Cha Chicken

Ingredients

- » **Four 6- to 8-ounce skinless, boneless chicken breast fillets**
- » **1 lime, zested and juiced, divided**
- » **1 orange, zested and juiced, divided**
- » **¼ cup olive oil, divided**
- » **2 teaspoons minced garlic**
- » **¼ cup chopped fresh oregano**
- » **1 teaspoon ground cumin**
- » **½ teaspoon ground cayenne pepper**
- » **Salt and black pepper**
- » **1 sweet onion**
- » **1 red bell pepper**
- » **1 orange, peeled**
- » **2 large russet potatoes**
- » **Citrus Avocado Salsa, recipe on facing page 19**

1. Preheat the oven to 425°F and grease or line your sheet pan. Arrange the chicken on the pan and drizzle with the lime juice, 2 tablespoons of the orange juice, and 2 tablespoons of the oil; toss well to coat the chicken. Sprinkle both sides of the meat evenly with the garlic, oregano, cumin, cayenne pepper, a big pinch each of salt and black pepper, and the zest of both the lime and the orange.

2. Slice the onion, bell pepper, and whole peeled orange into a bowl. Cut each potato into six wedges and add them to the bowl. Drizzle with the remaining 2 tablespoons of oil and a pinch each of salt and black pepper and toss to coat; arrange the wedges around the chicken pieces in the pan, keeping the potatoes in a single layer. Bake for 40 to 45 minutes, drizzling with oil halfway through if needed, until the chicken is done (165°F) and the potatoes are tender and golden.

3. While the food bakes, prepare the Citrus Avocado Salsa.

4. Serve the chicken and vegetables with the Citrus Avocado Salsa.

Citrus Avocado Salsa

Peel and dice 1 avocado and 1 orange and toss into a bowl. Seed and finely chop 1 jalapeño and add it to the bowl along with 1 cup of chopped fresh cilantro, 1 tablespoon of orange juice, and a pinch of flaky sea salt; stir to combine.

Brown Sugar Chicken

Serves 4

Ingredients

- » 2 small butternut squash, halved lengthwise and seeds removed
- » 3 tablespoons coconut oil, divided
- » 2 to 3 tablespoons pure maple syrup
- » ¾ teaspoon ground nutmeg
- » ¾ teaspoon ground cinnamon
- » 1½ teaspoons coarse salt
- » ¼ cup brown sugar
- » 4 chicken hindquarters
- » 1 pound cauliflower florets
- » 1 teaspoon garlic salt
- » Black pepper to taste
- » Parsley for garnish

1. Preheat the oven to 400°F and grease or line your sheet pan. Set the squash halves on the prepared pan, cut sides up. Brush 1 tablespoon of the oil over the cut sides, drizzle with the maple syrup, and sprinkle with the nutmeg, cinnamon, and coarse salt.

2. Rub the brown sugar evenly into all sides of the chicken and arrange on the pan. Place the cauliflower on the pan, drizzle with the remaining 2 tablespoons of oil, and sprinkle with garlic salt and black pepper; toss to coat and arrange in a single layer. Bake 30 to 40 minutes or until the chicken is done (165°F) and the squash and cauliflower are tender.

3. Remove the pan from the oven and heat the broiler. Broil the food for a few minutes until caramelized and lightly charred in places. Garnish as desired.

Jumbo Chicken Pot Pie

Ingredients

- » **3 sheets frozen puff pastry, thawed**
- » **One 14-ounce bag frozen pearl onions**
- » **1 rotisserie chicken, shredded**
- » **2 carrots, thinly sliced**
- » **2 celery ribs, thinly sliced**
- » **Salt and black pepper**
- » **Two 12-ounce jars chicken gravy**
- » **1 egg**

1. Preheat the oven to 400°F and grease or line your sheet pan. Dump the frozen pearl onions on the prepared pan. Arrange the rotisserie chicken, carrots, and celery in a single layer on the pan; season generously with salt and black pepper. Drizzle the chicken gravy evenly over the food.

2. On a lightly floured work surface, stack two of the pastry sheets on top of each other and roll them out to 15" square; cut into 1" strips. Fold the remaining pastry sheet in half and roll it out to 7" x 15", then cut into 1" strips. Arrange all the strips crosswise over the filling, overlapping them so most of the filling is covered. Trim off any overhang from the sides of the pan.

3. Whisk the egg with a splash of water and brush the mixture over the pastry. Bake 35 to 40 minutes, until the pastry is deep golden brown.

4. Let stand 5 minutes before serving.

Serves 8

Chicken Bruschetta

Serves 4

Ingredients

- » ⅓ cup balsamic vinegar
- » ¼ cup olive oil
- » 2 teaspoons minced garlic
- » ½ teaspoon salt
- » ½ teaspoon black pepper
- » ¼ teaspoon dried oregano
- » ¼ teaspoon red pepper flakes
- » 4 boneless, skinless chicken breasts (about 1¾ pounds)
- » Bruschetta, recipe on facing page 23
- » ¾ pound tiny yellow potatoes

- » 1 parsnip
- » 1 yellow summer squash
- » A big handful of baby carrots
- » ⅓ cup grated Parmesan cheese
- » Softened butter
- » 8 small slices French bread
- » Basil, for garnish

1. In a big shallow bowl, whisk together the vinegar, oil, garlic, salt, black pepper, oregano, and red pepper flakes. Lay the chicken in the mixture, toss to coat, and marinate in the refrigerator for 1 hour. Meanwhile, make the Bruschetta and set aside until needed.

2. Preheat the oven to 425°F and grease or line your sheet pan. Cut the potatoes in half. Cut the parsnip in half crosswise; cut the narrower end in half lengthwise and the wider end into four lengthwise slices. Cut the squash in half crosswise, then into lengthwise quarters. Arrange the cut-up vegetables and carrots in the pan in a single layer. Place the marinated chicken on top of the vegetables and pour the marinade evenly over everything. Bake for 20 minutes.

3. Spoon some of the pan juices over the chicken, then sprinkle the Parmesan evenly over the meat. Spoon about half the Bruschetta around the chicken. Butter the bread slices and lean them against the rim of the pan. Bake an additional 20 to 25 minutes, until the chicken is done (165°F), and the bread is lightly toasted.

4. Serve the bread and the remaining Bruschetta alongside the chicken and vegetables. Garnish as desired.

Serves
4

Cashew Chicken

Ingredients

- » ⅓ cup soy sauce
- » 1 tablespoon hoisin sauce
- » 1 tablespoon apple cider vinegar
- » 2 tablespoons honey
- » 1 teaspoon toasted sesame oil
- » ½ teaspoon minced fresh ginger
- » 2 teaspoons minced garlic
- » 2 tablespoons cornstarch
- » ½ cup water

- » 1½ pounds boneless, skinless chicken thighs
- » Salt and black pepper to taste
- » 1 head broccoli
- » 1 red bell pepper
- » 1 green bell pepper
- » ¾ cup roasted unsalted cashews
- » Toasted sesame seeds* and sliced green onion
- » Two 8.8-ounce packages ready-to-eat brown rice and quinoa combination

1. Preheat the oven to 400°F and grease or line your sheet pan. In a small saucepan over medium heat, whisk together the soy sauce, hoisin sauce, vinegar, honey, oil, ginger, garlic, cornstarch, and water until combined. Heat until the sauce thickens and bubbles, stirring often, then remove from the heat.

2. Cut the chicken into 1" cubes and toss them onto the prepared pan; sprinkle with salt and black pepper and drizzle with half of the sauce mixture, tossing to coat. Bake for 8 minutes.

3. Meanwhile, cut the broccoli into florets and cut the bell peppers into chunks. Add the vegetables and the cashews to the hot pan, season with salt and black pepper, drizzle with a little of the remaining sauce, and stir everything together. Bake about 20 minutes more, until the chicken is no longer pink.

4. Remove the pan from the oven, drizzle with the remaining sauce, and sprinkle with the toasted sesame seeds and green onion.

5. Heat the brown rice and quinoa combination according to the package directions, divide into serving bowls, and spoon the chicken and vegetable mixture over the top.

*To toast the sesame seeds, place them in a dry skillet over medium heat for about 6 minutes or until golden brown, stirring occasionally.

Lemon-Parm Chicken

Ingredients

- » **1 egg**
- » **2 tablespoons lemon juice**
- » **1½ teaspoons chopped fresh parsley**
- » **4 teaspoons minced garlic, divided**
- » **Salt and black pepper**
- » **4 boneless, skinless chicken breasts (about 1¾ pounds)**

- » **½ cup dry breadcrumbs**
- » **⅓ cup grated Parmesan cheese**
- » **1 pound tiny yellow potatoes**
- » **1 pound fresh green beans**
- » **½ cup butter**
- » **2 lemons, divided**

1. In a shallow pan, whisk together the egg, lemon juice, parsley, 2 teaspoons of the garlic, and ½ teaspoon each of the salt and black pepper. Coat both sides of the chicken with the egg mixture, then let marinate for 30 minutes.

2. Preheat the oven to 400°F and grease or line your sheet pan. On a plate, mix the breadcrumbs and cheese. Dredge the chicken pieces in the breadcrumb mixture, pressing lightly to evenly coat. Arrange the chicken on the prepared pan and spritz the top of the chicken pieces with cooking spray. Quarter the potatoes and arrange them around one side of the chicken. Arrange the beans on the other side.

3. Melt the butter and mix with the remaining 2 teaspoons of garlic, plus salt and black pepper to taste. Pour half the mixture over the potatoes and the other half over the beans; toss to coat and bake for 15 to 18 minutes.

4. Remove the pan from the oven and heat the broiler. Slice one of the lemons and add the slices to the pan. Broil the food for 10 minutes or until the chicken is done (165°F) and the potatoes and beans are tender.

5. Cut the remaining lemon in half and squeeze some of its juice over the food.

Serves
4

Moroccan Chicken

Ingredients

- » ¼ cup olive oil
- » 2 tablespoons honey
- » 2 teaspoons ground cumin
- » 1 teaspoon ground coriander
- » 1 teaspoon ground ginger
- » 1 teaspoon ground cayenne pepper or paprika
- » 1 tablespoon minced garlic
- » 3 pounds chicken pieces
- » 1 red onion, quartered
- » 1 pound tiny red potatoes, halved
- » 1¼ cups dried apricots
- » Cool Zhoug Sauce, recipe on facing page 27
- » Coarsely chopped pistachios
- » Mint and cilantro for garnish

1. Preheat the oven to 350°F and grease or line your sheet pan. In a small bowl, stir together the oil, honey, cumin, coriander, ginger, cayenne, and garlic. In a big bowl, combine the chicken, onion, and potatoes and drizzle with ¾ of the honey mixture; toss to coat. Arrange in a single layer on the prepared pan; bake for 35 minutes.

2. Toss the dried apricots with the remaining honey mixture. Add to the pan and bake 15 to 20 minutes longer, until the chicken is done (165°F). Meanwhile, make the Cool Zhoug Sauce and set it aside.

3. Sprinkle the food with pistachios and garnish as desired. Serve with the Cool Zhoug Sauce.

Cool Zhoug Sauce

Mix ¾ cup chopped cilantro, ½ cup chopped mint, ¼ teaspoon each ground cumin and ginger, the zest and juice of 1 lime, ¼ cup olive oil, a little honey, and sea salt to taste.

Cranberry Chicken Wraps

Makes 4

Ingredients

- » **1 tablespoon vegetable oil**
- » **¾ pound boneless chicken breast, cut into small pieces**
- » **One 5.3-ounce container plain Greek yogurt**
- » **¼ cup plus 1 tablespoon mayonnaise**
- » **1½ teaspoons Dijon mustard**
- » **⅓ cup dried cranberries**
- » **2 celery ribs, diced**
- » **1 red onion, finely chopped**
- » **Zest from 2 lemons**
- » **1½ teaspoons dried tarragon**
- » **One 6-ounce can water chestnuts, drained and chopped**
- » **½ cup chopped walnuts, toasted if desired**
- » **Salt and black pepper to taste**
- » **Four 10" flour tortillas**
- » **Alfalfa sprouts**

1. Heat the oil in a skillet and add the chicken, cooking until no longer pink; set aside.

2. In a medium bowl, combine the yogurt, mayonnaise, mustard, dried cranberries, celery, onion, lemon zest, tarragon, water chestnuts, and walnuts; stir in the set-aside chicken and season with salt and black pepper.

3. Heat the tortillas according to the package directions. Divide the chicken mixture among the tortillas and add some sprouts.

Mexican Chicken Soup

Serves 8

Ingredients

» **2 tablespoons olive oil**
» **¾ cup chopped frozen onion**
» **1 red bell pepper, chopped**
» **1 jalapeño pepper, seeded and finely chopped**
» **1 tablespoon smoked paprika**
» **1 teaspoon red pepper flakes**
» **Salt and black pepper to taste**
» **3 cups shredded rotisserie chicken**
» **2 cups frozen corn kernels**
» **4 cups chicken broth**
» **One 15-ounce can diced tomatoes with garlic and olive oil**
» **Once 15-ounce can black beans, drained and rinsed**
» **Your favorite toppings (we used sour cream, feta cheese, cilantro, jalapeños, and tortilla chips)**

1. Heat the oil in a big saucepan over medium-high heat. Add the onion, bell pepper, and jalapeño. Cook for a few minutes then add the smoked paprika, red pepper flakes, salt, and black pepper. Cook and stir briefly. Add the chicken, corn, broth, tomatoes, and black beans. Bring to a boil; cover, reduce heat, and simmer for 15 minutes.

2. Top each serving as desired.

Chicken Curry Shot

Serves 1

Ingredients

- » **1 tablespoon thinly sliced green onion**
- » **½ teaspoon curry powder**
- » **⅓ cup water**
- » **2½ tablespoons quick-cooking couscous**
- » **2½ tablespoons partially thawed peas**
- » **¼ cup cubed cooked chicken**
- » **2 tablespoons mayonnaise**
- » **2 tablespoons chopped red bell pepper**
- » **2 tablespoons sweet mango chutney**
- » **Pita chips, for serving**

1. In a greased 10-ounce mug, mix the green onion, curry powder, water, and couscous. Microwave on high until it boils. Stir in the peas, chicken, mayonnaise, red bell pepper, and sweet mango chutney. Cover with vented plastic wrap and cook at 70% power for 3 minutes, until tender.

2. Serve with pita chips.

BBQ Chicken & Twirls

Ingredients

- **2 cups shredded rotisserie chicken**
- **8 ounces uncooked twirly pasta**
- **One 15-ounce can petite diced tomatoes or 10-ounce can diced tomatoes with green chiles**
- **2½ cups chicken broth**
- **Salt, black pepper, paprika, and garlic powder to taste**
- **BBQ sauce**
- **1 cup shredded Monterey Jack cheese**
- **Bacon bits and sliced green onions, for serving**

1. In a big skillet, combine the shredded chicken, pasta, diced tomatoes or diced tomatoes with green chiles, chicken broth, and salt, black pepper, paprika, and garlic powder to taste. Cover and bring to a boil over high heat.

2. Reduce heat to low and simmer for 15 minutes, until the pasta is tender and most of the liquid has evaporated, stirring twice.

3. Drizzle with the BBQ sauce and sprinkle the shredded Monterey Jack cheese over the top. Cover the skillet and cook over low heat until the cheese melts.

4. Top with the bacon bits and sliced green onions for serving.

Serves 4

Flamin' Buffalo Chicken Enchiladas

Serves 6-8

Ingredients

» **Butter**
» **4 cups shredded rotisserie chicken**
» **One 8-ounce package cream cheese, softened**
» **¼ teaspoon ground cumin**
» **2 cups shredded cheddar cheese, divided**
» **1 cup hot sauce, divided**
» **1 bunch green onions, thinly sliced, white and green parts separated**
» **3 tablespoons water**
» **Fifteen to sixteen 6" corn tortillas**
» **3 tablespoons crumbled blue cheese, divided**
» **Blue cheese dressing**

1. Preheat your oven to 400°F and butter a 9" x 13" baking pan.

2. In a big bowl, mix the chicken, cream cheese, cumin, 1 cup of the cheddar cheese, ⅓ cup of the hot sauce, and the white parts of the green onions. In a small bowl, mix 3 tablespoons of melted butter, the remaining ⅔ cup of hot sauce, and the water.

3. In batches, heat the tortillas in the microwave according to the package directions and keep them warm. Spoon about ¼ cup of the chicken mixture down the center of each tortilla; roll them up and arrange them side by side in the prepared pan, seam side down. Pour the butter mixture evenly over the top and sprinkle with 2 tablespoons of the blue cheese and the remaining 1 cup of cheddar cheese. Bake until hot and bubbly, 15 to 20 minutes.

4. Before serving, drizzle the enchiladas with the dressing and sprinkle with the remaining 1 tablespoon of blue cheese and the green parts of the green onions.

Chopped Salad with Jalapeño Dressing

Ingredients

- » ¼ cup pickled jalapeños, finely chopped
- » ¼ cup mayonnaise
- » ¼ cup ranch dressing or sour cream
- » 2 tablespoons cilantro, chopped
- » 1 tablespoon lime juice
- » ½ teaspoon paprika
- » 1 to 2 tablespoons milk or half-and-half
- » One 15-ounce can yellow hominy, drained, rinsed, and patted dry
- » Cayenne pepper to taste
- » 4 cups Romaine lettuce, chopped
- » Grape tomatoes, halved
- » 1 cup rotisserie chicken or leftover cooked chicken
- » 1 mango, peeled, seeded, and sliced
- » 1 avocado, peeled, seeded, and sliced
- » 1 bell pepper (any color), sliced
- » Queso fresco or feta cheese, crumbled
- » Pumpkin seeds (pepitas)

1. In a mason jar or other lidded container, combine the pickled jalapeños, mayonnaise, ranch dressing or sour cream, cilantro, lime juice, and paprika. Pour in enough milk to reach the consistency you like. Cover, shake, and chill until serving time.

2. In a medium skillet, heat the hominy over low heat until just beginning to brown, stirring occasionally; sprinkle with cayenne pepper.

3. On a big tray, arrange the lettuce, hominy, tomatoes, chicken, mango, avocado, and bell pepper. Serve with the chilled dressing, queso fresco or feta, and pumpkin seeds alongside.

Serves 2

Serves
4

If you're not in
the mood for
biscuits, serve
this delicious
classic over rice!

Chicken à la RV

Ingredients

- » **1 cup fresh mushroom, sliced**
- » **½ green bell pepper, minced**
- » **½ cup butter**
- » **½ cup flour**
- » **1 teaspoon salt**
- » **¼ teaspoon pepper**
- » **1½ teaspoons chicken bouillon**

- » **1½ cups milk**
- » **1½ cups hot water**
- » **4 boneless, skinless chicken breast halves, cooked and chopped**
- » **4 refrigerator biscuits, baked as directed on package**

1. In a medium skillet or pan over medium heat, sauté the sliced mushrooms and minced green peppers in butter. Cook until the vegetables are softened, about 5 minutes, and remove from the heat.

2. Stir in the flour, salt, and pepper. Return to low heat and cook until the mixture is bubbly, stirring constantly. Remove from the heat and stir in chicken bouillon, milk, and water. Return to the heat and bring to a boil for 1 minute, stirring constantly. Stir in the chopped chicken and cook until heated throughout.

3. To serve, set one split biscuit on each plate and spread additional butter over the top. Spoon a generous amount of the hot chicken mixture over the biscuits on each plate.

One-Pot Lasagna

Serves 6

Ingredients

- » **1 tablespoon vegetable oil**
- » **1 pound ground turkey**
- » **½ teaspoon garlic powder**
- » **½ teaspoon onion powder**
- » **½ teaspoon red pepper flakes**
- » **Salt and black pepper to taste**
- » **6 ounces mini lasagna noodles (mafalda)**
- » **One 24-ounce jar marinara sauce**
- » **2 cups chicken stock**
- » **½ cup shredded mozzarella cheese**
- » **¼ cup grated Parmesan cheese**
- » **¾ cup cottage cheese**

1. Heat the oil in a medium saucepan over medium-high heat. Add the ground turkey and cook until it's no longer pink, crumbling it while it cooks; drain and return to the saucepan.

2. Stir in the garlic powder, onion powder, red pepper flakes, salt, and black pepper and cook for a minute or two. Stir in the noodles, marinara sauce, and stock. Bring to a boil, cover, and simmer for 20 minutes until the noodles are tender, stirring often.

3. Remove the pan from the heat and stir in half the mozzarella and Parmesan cheeses. Drop the cottage cheese in blobs over the top and sprinkle with the remaining mozzarella and Parmesan. Cover and let stand off the heat until the cheese is melted. Stir gently before serving.

Serves 4-6

Chicken Quesadillas

Ingredients

- » 3 cups chicken, cooked and chopped
- » One 1¼-ounce envelope fajita seasoning
- » 1 tablespoon vegetable oil
- » 2 green bell peppers, chopped
- » 2 red bell peppers, chopped
- » 1 onion, chopped
- » Ten 10" flour tortillas
- » 1 cup shredded Cheddar cheese
- » 1 cup shredded Monterey Jack cheese

1. In a large skillet over medium heat, combine the chicken, fajita seasoning, green bell pepper, red bell pepper, and onions. Cook for 10 minutes, stirring occasionally, until the vegetables are tender.

2. Divide the chicken mixture evenly over half of each tortilla. Sprinkle each tortilla with some of the Cheddar cheese and some of the Monterey Jack cheese. Fold each tortilla in half to enclose the filling. Clean out the skillet.

3. Add oil to the skillet and place the folded tortillas in, working in batches as needed. Brown one side then flip after 2 to 4 minutes to brown the other side. The cheese should be melted.

Turkey Fried Rice

Ingredients

- » **1¼ pounds boneless, skinless turkey breast cut into 1" cubes**
- » **Salt and black pepper**
- » **2 eggs**
- » **One 15-ounce can peas and carrots combination, drained**
- » **½ white onion, coarsely chopped**
- » **2 cups ready-to-eat rice**
- » **⅓ cup soy sauce**
- » **3 tablespoons sesame oil**
- » **Green onions, chopped**
- » **Orange juice for serving**

1. Preheat the oven to 400°F and grease or line your sheet pan. Place turkey in a single layer on the prepared pan; season with salt and black pepper. Bake for 5 minutes. In a small bowl, whisk the eggs and pour onto the hot pan and bake 3 to 4 minutes, until the egg is cooked. Use a fork to break the egg into tiny pieces.

2. Add the peas and carrots combination, white onion, and rice to the hot pan. Drizzle the soy sauce and sesame oil over the food, toss to coat, and arrange in a single layer; sprinkle with green onions. Bake an additional 10 to 15 minutes or until the turkey is no longer pink.

3. Toss the rice mixture and drizzle with a little orange juice before serving.

Serves 4

Fruited Balsamic Chicken

Serves 4-6

Ingredients

- » 2 tablespoons olive oil
- » Two 5-ounce to 6-ounce boneless, skinless chicken breast halves
- » ½ cup chopped onion
- » Salt and black pepper to taste
- » ½ teaspoon minced garlic
- » 2½ tablespoons balsamic vinegar
- » 1½ teaspoons honey
- » 1 medium peach (ripe but still firm), sliced
- » 1 cup pitted sweet cherries
- » Sliced fresh basil, optional

1. Heat the oil in a medium skillet over medium heat. Add the chicken breasts and dump the onion around the outer edge of the skillet; season with salt and pepper. Fry the chicken a few minutes on each side, until golden brown, stirring the onion often. Transfer the chicken to a plate.

2. Add the garlic to the skillet with the onion and heat for 30 seconds. Stir in the vinegar and cook a couple of minutes, until the liquid is reduced by about half. Stir in the honey, then add the peaches and cherries, tossing to coat.

3. Return the chicken and any accumulated juices to the skillet, nestling the pieces among the fruit; season everything with a little more salt and pepper. Cover the skillet, reduce the heat to medium-low, and simmer for 7 or 8 minutes, until the internal temperature of the chicken reaches 165°F. Top with basil, if desired.

Honey Dijon Chicken

Ingredients

- » ⅓ cup Dijon mustard
- » 3 tablespoons honey
- » 3 tablespoons snipped fresh parsley
- » 4 boneless, skinless chicken breast halves
- » Salt and black pepper to taste

1. Preheat your grill to medium heat and brush the grill grate with olive oil. In a small bowl, stir together Dijon mustard, honey, and fresh parsley; set aside.

2. One at a time, place the chicken breast halves between two pieces of waxed paper or plastic wrap and flatten them with the flat side of a meat mallet to an even thickness of about ½".

3. Grill the chicken for 3 minutes; flip and brush generously with the set-aside mustard mixture. Grill 2 to 3 minutes more or until golden and the juices just begin to run clear.

4. Transfer the chicken to a platter and cover loosely with foil; let stand 5 minutes. Season with salt and black pepper.

Serves
4

Serves 4

Chicken Enchilada Skillet

Ingredients

- » **One 10-ounce can tomatoes with green chiles**
- » **1 cup enchilada sauce**
- » **1 cup black beans, drained and rinsed**
- » **2 boneless, skinless chicken breast halves**

- » **Salt to taste**
- » **4 corn tortillas, cut into bite-sized pieces**
- » **½ cup shredded Monterey Jack cheese**
- » **Green onion, avocado, tomatoes, and sour cream, for serving**

1. In a medium oven-safe skillet over medium heat, combine the tomatoes with green chiles, enchilada sauce, and black beans; bring to a simmer. Season the chicken breast halves with salt; add to the skillet and cook over low heat for 20 minutes or until done, turning once.

2. Preheat your broiler. Shred the chicken and stir in the corn tortillas. Cover and simmer for 5 minutes. Uncover, sprinkle with Monterey Jack cheese, and broil a minute or two until the cheese melts.

3. Serve hot topped with green onion, avocado, tomatoes, and sour cream.

Chinese Turkey Wraps

Ingredients

- » ¼ cup toasted sesame oil, divided
- » 1½ pounds boneless, skinless turkey breast, cut into 1" pieces
- » 1½ teaspoons minced garlic
- » One 14-ounce can bean sprouts, drained
- » One 8-ounce can sliced water chestnuts, drained
- » 2½ cups coleslaw mix or shredded cabbage, divided
- » ⅓ cup each hoisin sauce and soy sauce
- » ¼ cup brown sugar
- » 2 tablespoons cornstarch
- » Eight 8" flour tortillas, warmed
- » 1 tomato, diced
- » Chow mein noodles

1. Heat 2 tablespoons of the oil in a big skillet over medium-high heat. Add the turkey and garlic and cook for 8 to 10 minutes or until done, stirring frequently; pour off half the accumulated liquid in the skillet. Stir in the bean sprouts, water chestnuts, and 2 cups of the coleslaw mix. Cook about 4 minutes.

2. In a small bowl, whisk together the hoisin sauce, soy sauce, brown sugar, cornstarch, and the remaining 2 tablespoons of oil; pour into the skillet and bring to a boil. Cook for 1 minute to thicken.

3. Spoon some turkey mixture onto each tortilla and divide the remaining ½ cup of coleslaw mix over the top. Sprinkle with the tomato and chow mein noodles. Roll up and enjoy!

Makes 8

Makes 8-10

Chicken Caesar Sliders

Ingredients

- » ¾ cup Caesar salad dressing
- » ½ cup grated Parmesan cheese plus more for serving
- » 1 handful fresh parsley, chopped
- » ½ teaspoon black pepper
- » 3 cups shredded rotisserie chicken
- » Slider buns and lettuce, for serving

1. In a medium saucepan, stir together the salad dressing, grated Parmesan cheese, fresh parsley, and black pepper. Stir in the shredded rotisserie chicken. Cover and cook over low heat until the mixture is nice and hot, stirring often.

2. Serve on slider buns with lettuce and a little extra Parmesan.

Salads to Go

Ingredients

- » **3 cups chopped fresh kale or other sturdy greens**
- » **1½ cups packaged broccoli slaw**
- » **1 cup chopped cooked chicken**
- » **⅓ cup dried cranberries**
- » **1 to 2 tablespoons salad dressing**
- » **2 to 3 tablespoons sunflower kernels or pepitas**

1. In a big bowl, mix the kale or sturdy greens, broccoli slaw, cooked chicken, and dried cranberries.

2. Pour your favorite salad dressing into the bottom of four wide-mouth 1-pint mason jars or other lidded containers. Divide the salad mixture among the jars, seal with lids, and refrigerate.

3. When you're ready to eat, give the salads a quick stir and toss the sunflower kernels or pepitas on top.

Serves 4

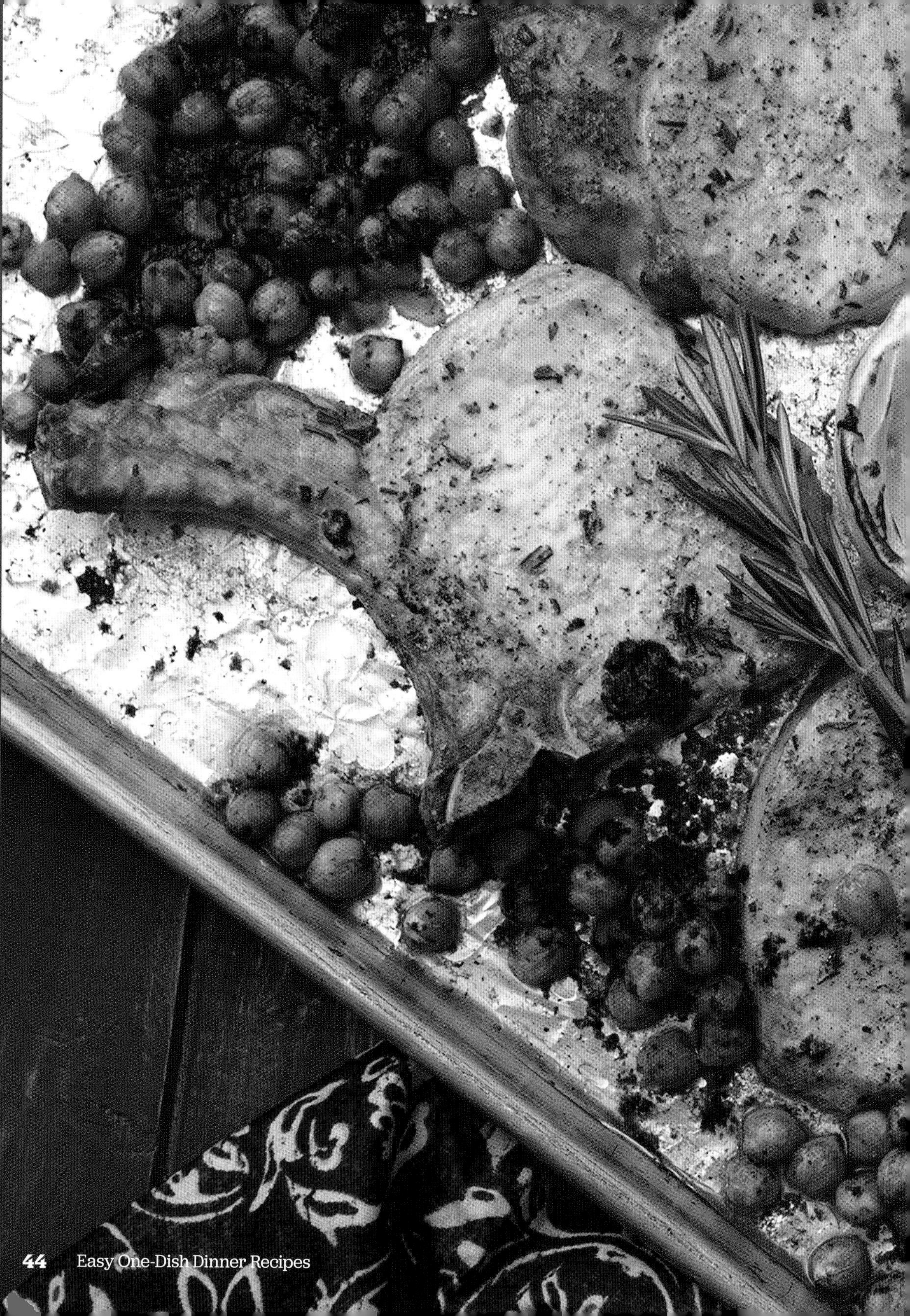

Pork in a Snap

From flavorful tenderloins, hams, and pork chops to ever-popular sausage, deli meat, and bacon, pork adds savor to any dish! Pork is perfect on its own, but it really shines when mixed with flavorful seafood or sweet fruits and vegetables. Try something a little different tonight with these quick pork-based treats.

Tenderloin with Roasted Veggies

Serves 4

Ingredients

- » **2 tablespoons olive oil**
- » **2½ tablespoons honey**
- » **3½ tablespoons balsamic vinegar**
- » **1½ teaspoons minced garlic**
- » **1 teaspoon black pepper**
- » **2 teaspoons finely chopped fresh rosemary, divided**
- » **One 1 to 1¼ pound pork tenderloin**
- » **3 cups halved Brussels sprouts (quartered if large)**
- » **2 parsnips, peeled and sliced ¼" thick**
- » **3 large carrots, sliced ¼" thick**
- » **1 red onion, cut into 8 wedges**
- » **Salt to taste**

1. Preheat the oven to 425°F and grease or line your sheet pan. In a small bowl, combine the oil, honey, vinegar, garlic, black pepper, and 1¾ teaspoons of the rosemary; whisk well.

2. Use paper towels to pat the tenderloin dry and set it on the prepared pan. Brush about 2 tablespoons of the oil mixture over all sides of the meat and sprinkle with the remaining ¼ teaspoon of rosemary. Arrange the Brussels sprouts, parsnips, carrots, and onion around the meat and drizzle the remaining oil mixture over the vegetables; toss to coat and season with salt. Bake for 30 to 45 minutes or until the meat is cooked (145°F) and the vegetables are crisp-tender.

3. Remove the pan from the oven, preheat the broiler, and set the pan under the heat for a few minutes to brown. Let the food rest for 5 minutes before slicing the meat.

Spicy Cajun Shrimp & Sausage

Ingredients

- » **1½ pounds tiny potatoes**
- » **1 tablespoon olive oil**
- » **½ cup butter, plus more for serving, melted**
- » **1 teaspoon smoked paprika**
- » **½ teaspoon ground cayenne pepper**
- » **½ teaspoon dried thyme**
- » **½ teaspoon salt**
- » **½ teaspoon black pepper**
- » **½ teaspoon garlic powder**
- » **4 ears sweet corn, cut into 2" chunks**
- » **1 pound smoked Andouille sausage, sliced ¼" thick**
- » **1½ pounds uncooked shrimp, peeled and deveined**
- » **Hot sauce and lemon wedges for serving**
- » **Parsley for garnish**

1. Preheat the oven to 425°F and grease or line your sheet pan. Put the potatoes on the prepared pan, drizzle with the oil, and toss them to coat. Stir together ½ cup of the butter with the paprika, cayenne pepper, thyme, salt, black pepper, and garlic powder. Add the corn chunks to the pan and brush them with a little of the seasoned butter; set the remaining butter mixture aside. Bake for 20 to 25 minutes.

2. Remove the pan from the oven and add the sausage and shrimp. Brush the remaining seasoned butter evenly over the food and bake an additional 10 to 15 minutes or until the shrimp is cooked and everything is heated through.

3. Serve with hot sauce, lemon wedges, and extra melted butter. Garnish as desired.

Serves 6

Sweet Curry Chops

Serves
3

Ingredients

- » **4 teaspoons mild curry powder**
- » **1 teaspoon black pepper**
- » **1 teaspoon brown sugar**
- » **2 ½ teaspoons salt**
- » **1 small head cauliflower**
- » **3 small sweet potatoes**
- » **Three ¾" to 1" thick bone-in pork chops**
- » **2 ½ tablespoons olive oil**
- » **Sliced radishes and parsley for garnish**
- » **Simple Yogurt Sauce, recipe on facing page 49**

1. Arrange an oven rack in the top third of the oven and preheat oven to 450°F. Grease or line your sheet pan. Prepare the Simple Yogurt Sauce and refrigerate it until needed.

2. In a small bowl, stir together the curry powder, black pepper, brown sugar, and salt; set the mixture aside.

3. Cut the cauliflower into florets and cut the sweet potatoes in half lengthwise and arrange them on the prepared pan along with the pork chops. Drizzle the oil over the food, sprinkle everything with the curry mixture, and toss to coat.

4. Bake for 30 minutes or until the chops are cooked through (145°F) and the vegetables are fork-tender and deep brown underneath. If the chops finish cooking before the sweet potatoes, remove them to a plate and cover them with foil until the sweet potatoes are done.

5. Garnish as desired. Serve the food with the chilled Simple Yogurt Sauce.

Simple Yogurt Sauce

Whisk together ⅔ cups plain Greek yogurt, 1½ tablespoons lemon juice, ¼ teaspoon garlic powder, ½ teaspoon salt, and a pinch of black pepper.

Serves
4

Sausage & Greens

Ingredients

- » 1 pound ground mild sausage
- » 2 medium sweet potatoes
- » 1 orange bell pepper
- » ½ red onion
- » 3 tablespoons butter, melted

- » 1 tablespoon preferred seasoning (such as steak and chop seasoning)
- » 1 bunch kale
- » 8 eggs

1. Preheat the oven to 425°F and grease or line your sheet pan. Crumble the sausage onto one side of the prepared pan. Shred the sweet potatoes and spread out beside the sausage. Coarsely chop the bell pepper and red onion and toss them onto the sweet potato shreds. Pour melted butter over the vegetables, toss them to coat, and spread out evenly, leaving the sausage separate. Bake for 15 minutes.

2. Sprinkle the vegetables with your favorite seasoning. Remove and discard the thick stems from the kale and roughly chop the leaves; spread evenly over the vegetables. Crumble the sausage again and layer it on top of the kale; distributing the food to fill the pan. Bake about 3 minutes, until the kale just begins to wilt. Create eight wells in the food and crack an egg into each. Bake an additional 10 minutes or until the egg whites are set.

3. Season the eggs to taste and serve.

Mustard-Glazed Brats, Squash & Kale Chips

Ingredients

- » ¼ cup olive oil
- » ¼ cup spicy brown mustard
- » ¼ cup apple cider vinegar
- » 2 teaspoons honey
- » ½ teaspoon salt
- » ½ teaspoon black pepper

- » One 2-pound acorn squash, halved and sliced 1" thick, seeds discarded
- » 5 uncooked bratwursts
- » 2 Granny Smith apples, cored and cut into 8 wedges each
- » 4 cups coarsely chopped fresh kale (packed)

1. Preheat the oven to 425°F and grease or line your sheet pan. In a bowl, whisk together the oil, mustard, vinegar, honey, salt, and black pepper. Arrange the squash, bratwursts, and apples on the prepared pan. Remove 3 tablespoons of the mustard mixture from the bowl and brush it over the food; bake for 20 minutes.

2. Toss the kale with about 3 tablespoons of the remaining mustard mixture. Remove the pan from the oven and arrange the kale on top of the food. Bake 8 to 10 minutes more or until the kale is crisp, the bratwursts are done (160°F), and the squash is tender.

3. Serve the remaining mustard mixture alongside the food.

Serves 5

Serves 4

Chops & Chickpeas

Ingredients

- » **Fresh rosemary sprigs**
- » **4 tablespoons olive oil, divided**
- » **Zest and juice of ½ lemon**
- » **Four ¾" thick center-cut bone-in pork chops**
- » **Salt and black pepper**
- » **One 15-ounce can chickpeas, drained and rinsed**
- » **6 garlic cloves**
- » **½ cup sliced roasted red peppers**
- » **⅓ cup chicken broth**

1. Preheat the broiler and line your sheet pan. Chop the leaves from the fresh rosemary sprigs until you have 1 teaspoonful (reserve the stripped sprigs).

2. On the prepared pan, combine 1 tablespoon of the olive oil, the chopped rosemary, and the lemon zest and juice. Arrange the pork chops on the pan, turning them to coat both sides with the oil mixture; season generously with salt and black pepper.

3. In a bowl, stir together the chickpeas, garlic cloves, roasted red pepper slices, the stripped rosemary sprigs, the remaining 3 tablespoons of olive oil, and ½ teaspoon each of salt and black pepper and scatter the mixture around the chops; pour the chicken broth over the chickpeas. Broil 10 to 12 minutes, until the chops are cooked through (145°F), basting several times and rotating the pan halfway through.

4. Remove the stripped rosemary sprigs before serving.

Big Pan Jambalaya

Ingredients

- » **12 mini bell peppers**
- » **Half 14-ounce package kielbasa**
- » **3 tablespoons olive oil, divided**
- » **3¼ teaspoons Creole seasoning, divided**
- » **¾ pound medium uncooked shrimp, peeled and deveined**
- » **1 pint cherry tomatoes, halved**
- » **¾ teaspoon paprika**
- » **Two 8.8-ounce packages ready-to-eat rice**
- » **Salt and black pepper**
- » **Green onions, for serving**

1. Preheat the oven to 425°F and grease or line your sheet pan. Cut the mini bell peppers in half and thinly slice the kielbasa; toss everything onto the prepared pan. Drizzle with 2 tablespoons of olive oil and sprinkle with 1½ teaspoons of Creole seasoning. Bake for 8 minutes.

2. Meanwhile, in a bowl, combine the shrimp, cherry tomatoes, 1 tablespoon olive oil, ¾ teaspoon Creole seasoning, and paprika; toss to coat, add to the pan with the vegetables, and stir gently. Bake for 7 minutes. Add the rice, ½ teaspoon each salt and black pepper, and 1 teaspoon Creole seasoning and toss to combine. Bake a few minutes longer, until the rice is heated through, and the shrimp is done.

3. Sprinkle with the green onions.

Serves 4

Hasselback Ham with Rutabaga "Fries"

Serves 6

Ingredients

- » **One 2-pound boneless ham**
- » **6 slices Swiss cheese, halved**
- » **1 teaspoon minced garlic**
- » **½ teaspoon black pepper, divided**
- » **¼ cup butter, melted, divided**
- » **½ teaspoon salt, divided**
- » **One 1-pound rutabaga, cut into French fry shapes**
- » **1 pound asparagus, halved**
- » **Honey**
- » **Chives, for garnish**
- » **Grainy mustard, for serving**

1. Preheat the oven to 400°F; grease your sheet pan, set a 12" square piece of foil in the center, and set the ham on the foil. Make 12 even cuts through the top of the ham, without cutting through the bottom; place half a slice of cheese into each cut. In a big bowl, mix the garlic, ¼ teaspoon of the black pepper, and 2 tablespoons of the butter and brush the mixture all over the ham. Pull the foil up around the ham and cover tightly with more foil.

2. In the same bowl, stir together 1 tablespoon of the remaining butter, ¼ teaspoon of salt, and the remaining ¼ teaspoon of pepper. Add the rutabaga, toss to coat, and arrange in a single layer beside the ham. Bake for 45 minutes, then flip the fries over.

3. In the same bowl, combine the asparagus, the remaining 1 tablespoon of butter, and the remaining ¼ teaspoon of salt; toss to coat and arrange in the pan. Bake 12 to 15 minutes, until the ham is heated through (140°F) and the vegetables are fork-tender.

4. Drizzle the ham with honey, garnish as desired, and serve with mustard.

Big Sheet Bacon & Browns

Ingredients

- » One 20-ounce package refrigerated hash browns
- » ½ cup grated onion
- » 2 tablespoons melted butter
- » 1 tablespoon olive oil
- » 1 teaspoon garlic powder
- » 1 teaspoon paprika
- » Salt and black pepper to taste
- » 1 cup shredded cheddar cheese
- » 6 bacon strips
- » 6 eggs
- » Parmesan, Romano, or Asiago cheese
- » Parsley or chives, for garnish

1. Preheat the oven to 400°F and grease or line your sheet pan. Dump the hash browns onto the prepared pan and stir in the onion, melted butter, olive oil, garlic powder, paprika, and salt and black pepper to taste. Spread in an even layer and sprinkle with the cheddar cheese. Bake for 15 minutes, until the edges begin to brown. Remove the pan from the oven and create six wells in the hash browns.

2. Cut the bacon strips in half and line each well with two halves; crack an egg in the center of each. Sprinkle each egg with Parmesan, Romano, or Asiago cheese and season with salt and black pepper. Bake an additional 15 minutes or until the egg whites are set and the bacon is cooked.

3. Garnish with parsley or chives.

Serves 6

For crispier bacon, add it with the cheddar cheese so it bakes the entire time. Then add just the eggs to cook the last 15 minutes.

Serves 4

Smoked Sausage with Apples & Roots

Ingredients

- » 2 tablespoons olive oil
- » 2 tablespoons Dijon mustard
- » 2 tablespoons pure maple syrup
- » ¾ teaspoon fresh thyme leaves
- » One 12-ounce package smoked beef sausage
- » 2 Honeycrisp apples

- » 1 large sweet onion
- » 1 pound tiny yellow potatoes
- » ½ pound petite carrots
- » 2 parsnips, peeled and thinly sliced
- » Salt and black pepper
- » Sage leaves

1. Preheat the oven to 400°F and grease or line your sheet pan. In a big bowl, whisk together the olive oil, Dijon mustard, maple syrup, and thyme leaves. Cut the sausage, Honeycrisp apples, and sweet onion into 2" chunks and add them to the bowl along with the potatoes and carrots. Add the parsnips, toss everything to coat, and dump onto the prepared pan in a single layer.

2. Sprinkle generously with salt and black pepper. Lay several sage leaves on top of the food and bake for 50 minutes or until the vegetables are tender, stirring halfway through.

3. Remove the sage leaves before serving.

Potato Soup Solo

Ingredients

- » **1 cup cubed, unpeeled red potatos**
- » **⅓ cup chicken broth**
- » **¼ cup milk**
- » **1 bacon strip, cooked and crumbled**
- » **2 tablespoons shredded cheddar cheese**
- » **1 sliced green onion**
- » **Garlic salt and black pepper to taste**

1. Toss the potatoes into an ungreased 20-ounce mug; microwave on high for 2 minutes, stirring once. Add the chicken broth and milk. Microwave at 50% power for 4 to 5 minutes, until tender, stirring occasionally. Mash the potatoes lightly, leaving some small chunks.

2. Stir in the bacon, cheddar cheese, and green onion, then add garlic salt and black pepper to taste; stir before eating.

Serves
1

Cheesy Skillet Ravioli

Serves 4

Ingredients

» **1 tablespoon olive oil**
» **1 pound ground Italian sausage**
» **One 14.5-ounce can diced tomatoes with garlic and olive oil**
» **One 8-ounce can tomato sauce**
» **1 tablespoon tomato paste**
» **1 ½ teaspoons Italian seasoning**
» **1 teaspoon each garlic powder and onion powder**
» **Salt and black pepper to taste**
» **16 ounces frozen cheese ravioli**
» **1 cup water**
» **1 cup shredded mozzarella cheese**
» **⅓ cup grated Parmesan cheese**

1. Heat the oil in a big oven-safe skillet over medium-high heat. Add the sausage and cook until browned and crumbly; drain. Stir in the tomatoes, tomato sauce, tomato paste, and all the seasonings. Stir in the ravioli and water and bring to a boil.

2. Cover the skillet, reduce the heat, and simmer until the ravioli is tender, 10 to 12 minutes. Meanwhile, preheat the broiler.

3. Remove the skillet from the heat and stir; sprinkle with both cheeses. Transfer the skillet to the broiler and broil 6" away from the heat, until just golden brown, 2 to 4 minutes.

Kielbasa & Rice Single

Serves 1

Ingredients

- » ½ cup quick-cooking white rice
- » 2 tablespoons dry béarnaise sauce mix
- » 6 halved grape tomatoes
- » ½ teaspoon dried minced onion
- » ½ teaspoon chopped fresh chives
- » 3 tablespoons milk
- » ½ cup chicken broth
- » ⅓ cup diced fully cooked kielbasa

1. In a greased 14-ounce mug, stir together the rice, dry béarnaise sauce mix, grape tomatoes, dried minced onion, fresh chives, milk, chicken broth, and kielbasa. Microwave on high until bubbles form around the edge, then cook 1½ minutes more.

2. Cover with foil and let stand 5 minutes, until the rice is tender; stir before eating.

Skillet Chops & Apples

Serves **4**

Ingredients

» **4 boneless pork chops (¾" to 1" thick)**

» **Salt, black pepper, and garlic powder to taste**

» **1 tablespoon coconut oil**

» **4 Braeburn apples, peeled, cored and sliced**

» **1 small fennel bulb, cored and coarsely chopped**

» **½ yellow onion, thinly sliced**

» **1¼ cups chicken broth**

» **1 teaspoon ground cinnamon**

» **1 bunch fresh kale, stems removed and leaves chopped**

» **¼ cup raisins**

1. Preheat the oven to 400°F. Season both sides of the chops with salt, black pepper, and garlic powder. Heat the oil in a big oven-safe skillet over medium heat and add the chops; brown 2 to 3 minutes on each side. Add the apples, fennel, and onion. Cook until the apples begin to soften, stirring frequently.

2. Stir in the broth and cinnamon; simmer 2 to 3 minutes.

3. Transfer the skillet to the oven and bake uncovered for 7 to 10 minutes, until the chops test done with a meat thermometer (145°F). Remove the chops to a plate to keep them warm. Add the kale and raisins to the skillet; stir and cook until the kale is slightly wilted.

4. Return the chops to the skillet, heat through, and serve.

Cowboy Beans

Ingredients

- » 8 ounces smoked sausage links
- » 2 tablespoons butter
- » 1 ½ cups chopped onion
- » ¾ cup BBQ sauce
- » 2 tablespoons pure maple syrup
- » 2 tablespoons apple cider vinegar
- » ¼ cup water
- » One 16-ounce can red kidney beans, drained and rinsed

- » One 16-ounce can black beans, drained and rinsed
- » One 16-ounce can pinto beans, drained and rinsed
- » Seasoning to taste
- » Chopped green onions for topping

1. Slice the smoked sausage links to ½" thick and dump the pieces into a big skillet set over medium heat until evenly browned; remove the sausage from the skillet.

2. Melt the butter in the skillet and add the onion, cooking until softened. Stir in the BBQ sauce, maple syrup, apple cider vinegar, and water and bring to a boil. Add the beans and the browned sausages to the skillet; stir, cover the skillet, and simmer for at least 15 minutes, stirring occasionally. Season to taste.

3. Top with chopped green onions if you'd like.

Serves
8-12

Alfredo Bacon Pizza

Serves 4

Ingredients

» **One 13.8-ounce tube refrigerated pizza crust dough**

» **1 cup bacon-flavored or plain Alfredo sauce**

» **1¼ cups mozzarella cheese, shredded and divided**

» **One 10-ounce package frozen chopped spinach, thawed, drained and squeezed dry**

» **2 or 3 plum tomatoes, thinly sliced**

» **5 precooked bacon strips**

1. Heat the oven to 425°F. Coat a 12" pizza pan with cooking spray. Unroll the dough and press evenly into the prepped pan, making a small rim around the outer edge. Spread the sauce over the dough and sprinkle with ½ cup of the cheese. Arrange the spinach and tomatoes over the cheese. Cut the bacon strips into 1" pieces and arrange them over the top; sprinkle the remaining ¾ cup of cheese over all.

2. Bake for 15 minutes or until the crust is golden brown and the cheese is melted.

Hawaiian Pizza

Ingredients

- » **One 14-ounce tube refrigerated pizza crust dough**
- » **1 cup pizza sauce**
- » **Cooked Canadian bacon, chopped**
- » **One 8-ounce can pineapple chunks, drained**
- » **2 cups shredded mozzarella cheese**

1. Preheat the oven to 350°F.
2. Press the refrigerated pizza crust dough evenly onto a lightly greased 10" to 12" pizza pan. Spread the pizza sauce over the crust to within ½" from the edge. Sprinkle the Canadian bacon over the pizza sauce and spread the pineapple chunks over top. Sprinkle the shredded mozzarella cheese over the pizza.
3. Bake in the oven for 15 to 20 minutes or until the crust is lightly browned and the cheese is melted.

Serves
4-6

Serves
4-6

Camp Casserole

Ingredients

- » **1 small head Napa cabbage, shredded**
- » **6 slices bacon, cooked and crumbled**
- » **3 cups cooked ham, diced**
- » **1 medium onion, sliced**
- » **1 tablespoon butter**
- » **2 cups potatoes, cooked and diced**
- » **½ teaspoon paprika**
- » **Salt and pepper to taste**

1. In a large skillet over medium heat, place the shredded cabbage and ½ cup of water. Cook for 5 minutes, until the cabbage is tender. Drain the cabbage and set it aside.

2. Place the crumbled bacon and sliced onions in the skillet and cook until the onions are softened. Add the chopped ham, butter, cooked cabbage, and diced cooked potatoes. Mix well and season with paprika, salt, and pepper.

3. Cook until the mixture browns on the bottom, then turn over in the skillet and cook until the mixture is browned on the other side.

Hawaiian Ham Packs

Ingredients

» **1 large sweet potato, peeled and diced**
» **½ pound cubed fully cooked ham**
» **1 red bell pepper, cored and sliced into rings**
» **4 canned pineapple slices**
» **2 tablespoons butter**
» **2 tablespoons brown sugar**
» **Red pepper flakes to taste**

1. Preheat your grill to medium-high heat.

2. Divide the sweet potato pieces among two big pieces of foil spritzed with cooking spray. Layer the ham and bell pepper rings evenly over the sweet potatoes. Arrange two pineapple slices on each pack and top each with half the butter and half the brown sugar. Sprinkle with the red pepper flakes.

3. Wrap the foil around the food to make two tent packs, sealing the edges.

4. Set the foil packs on the grill grate and cover the grill. Cook for 20 minutes or until the sweet potatoes are tender, flipping the packs over during the last 5 minutes.

5. Open the packs carefully and enjoy.

Makes
6

Glazed Frank Kebabs

Ingredients

- » **4 hot dogs**
- » **2 ears of sweet corn, shucked**
- » **1 red onion**
- » **½ red bell pepper**
- » **½ green bell pepper**

- » **Cherry tomatoes**
- » **½ cup chili sauce**
- » **3 tablespoons brown sugar**
- » **2 tablespoons spicy brown mustard**

1. Slice the hot dogs and sweet corn into 1" pieces; slice the red onion into wedges. Cut the bell peppers into 1" pieces. Alternately thread pieces of hot dog, corn, onion, bell pepper, and a few cherry tomatoes on the skewers and set aside.

2. Combine the chili sauce, brown sugar, and spicy brown mustard in a bowl. Set the kebabs on a grate over medium-low heat; brush the skewers with some of the sauce mixture. Cover the food with foil and grill for about 5 minutes.

3. Continue to cook slowly until the vegetables are tender, rotating the kebabs every 5 minutes and brushing the skewers with more sauce.

4. Serve warm.

Big Bite Hoagies

Ingredients

- 6 pickled cherry peppers, finely chopped
- 1 teaspoon minced garlic
- 2 tablespoons pepperoncini peppers, chopped
- 1 tablespoon white wine vinegar
- 1 teaspoon sugar
- One 12" to 16" hoagie roll or unsliced Italian bread loaf

- 2 tablespoons mayonnaise
- Your favorite lunch meats and cheeses (we used salami, pickle and pimento loaf, and Canadian bacon with sliced provolone cheese)
- Sliced tomatoes, shredded lettuce, Italian seasoning, red wine vinegar, and olive oil, for serving

1. Toss the pickled cherry peppers in a bowl with the garlic, pepperoncini peppers, white wine vinegar, and sugar; stir well and set aside.

2. Split the hoagie roll or Italian bread loaf horizontally, without cutting all the way through. Spread with the mayonnaise. Layer on your favorite lunch meats and cheeses, then add sliced tomatoes, the pepper mixture, and shredded lettuce. Sprinkle with Italian seasoning and drizzle with a little red wine vinegar and olive oil. Close it up and take a big bite!

Serves 4-6

Serves
4

Stovetop Deli Pizza

Ingredients

- » **Olive oil**
- » **1 small yellow onion, thinly sliced**
- » **Salt and red pepper flakes**
- » **One 13.8-ounce tube refrigerated pizza crust**
- » **1 to 2 teaspoons minced garlic**
- » **8 ounces fresh mozzarella cheese, thinly sliced**
- » **4 ounces thinly sliced deli meats, chopped (we used salami, ham, and pastrami)**
- » **⅓ cup grated Parmesan cheese**
- » **Chopped fresh parsley**

1. Heat 1 tablespoon of oil in a 12" oven-safe skillet over medium-high heat. Add the onion and ½ teaspoon each of salt and red pepper flakes. Sauté until the onion softens and begins to brown; transfer to a plate. Preheat the broiler.

2. Brush the warm skillet with 1 tablespoon of oil. Unroll the pizza crust and press it into the bottom of the skillet. Reduce the heat to medium and cook 2 to 3 minutes, until the bottom is golden brown; flip the crust. Reduce the heat to medium-low and brush the browned side with oil; sprinkle with garlic and salt. Arrange the mozzarella slices on the crust and scatter the set-aside onions over top. Top with meats, Parmesan cheese, and red pepper flakes.

3. When the crust is golden brown on the bottom, broil the pizza 7" away from the heat for a few minutes, until the cheese is bubbly and the crust is brown. Top with parsley.

Cauliflower Chowder

Ingredients

- » **2 tablespoons butter**
- » **1 onion, diced**
- » **1 cup diced carrots**
- » **2 celery ribs, diced**
- » **1 teaspoon minced garlic**
- » **½ teaspoon ground thyme**
- » **¼ cup flour**
- » **Two 12-ounce bags cut cauliflower florets**
- » **4 cups chicken broth**
- » **4 fully cooked bacon strips, crumbled**
- » **2 bay leaves**
- » **1 cup heavy cream**
- » **Salt, black pepper, cayenne pepper, and red pepper flakes to taste**

1. Melt the butter in a big saucepan over medium-high heat. Add the onion, carrots, and celery; cook for 7 or 8 minutes. Stir in the garlic, thyme, and flour and cook 3 minutes longer.

2. Add the cauliflower florets to the saucepan with the vegetables. Slowly pour in the broth. Add the bacon and bay leaves; bring to a boil over medium-high heat. Reduce the heat and simmer for 10 to 12 minutes or until the vegetables are tender. Stir in the cream and seasonings.

3. Remember to remove those bay leaves, then dive in!

Serves 4

Easy Sausage & Chicken Stew

Serves
8

Ingredients

- » **3 tablespoons olive oil**
- » **5 mild bratwursts or sausage links, casings removed**
- » **1 onion, chopped**
- » **1 shallot, chopped**
- » **3 carrots, chopped**
- » **1 chicken breast, cooked and diced**
- » **5 red potatoes, cut into chunks**
- » **One 15-ounce can cannellini beans, drained and rinsed**
- » **One 49-ounce can chicken broth**
- » **¼ cup grated Parmesan cheese**
- » **1 teaspoon dried thyme leaves**
- » **Salt and black pepper to taste**
- » **5 cups chopped fresh kale**
- » **3 tablespoons flour**
- » **¾ cup cold water**

1. In a big saucepan, heat the oil over medium heat. Slice the sausages and add them to the hot oil along with the onion and shallot and cook until the sausages are done, stirring occasionally.

2. Add the carrots, chicken, potatoes, beans, broth, Parmesan, thyme, salt, and black pepper and simmer for 30 minutes, until everything is tender, stirring in the kale during the last 10 minutes.

3. In a small bowl, stir together the flour and water until smooth and stir into the stew until slightly thickened.

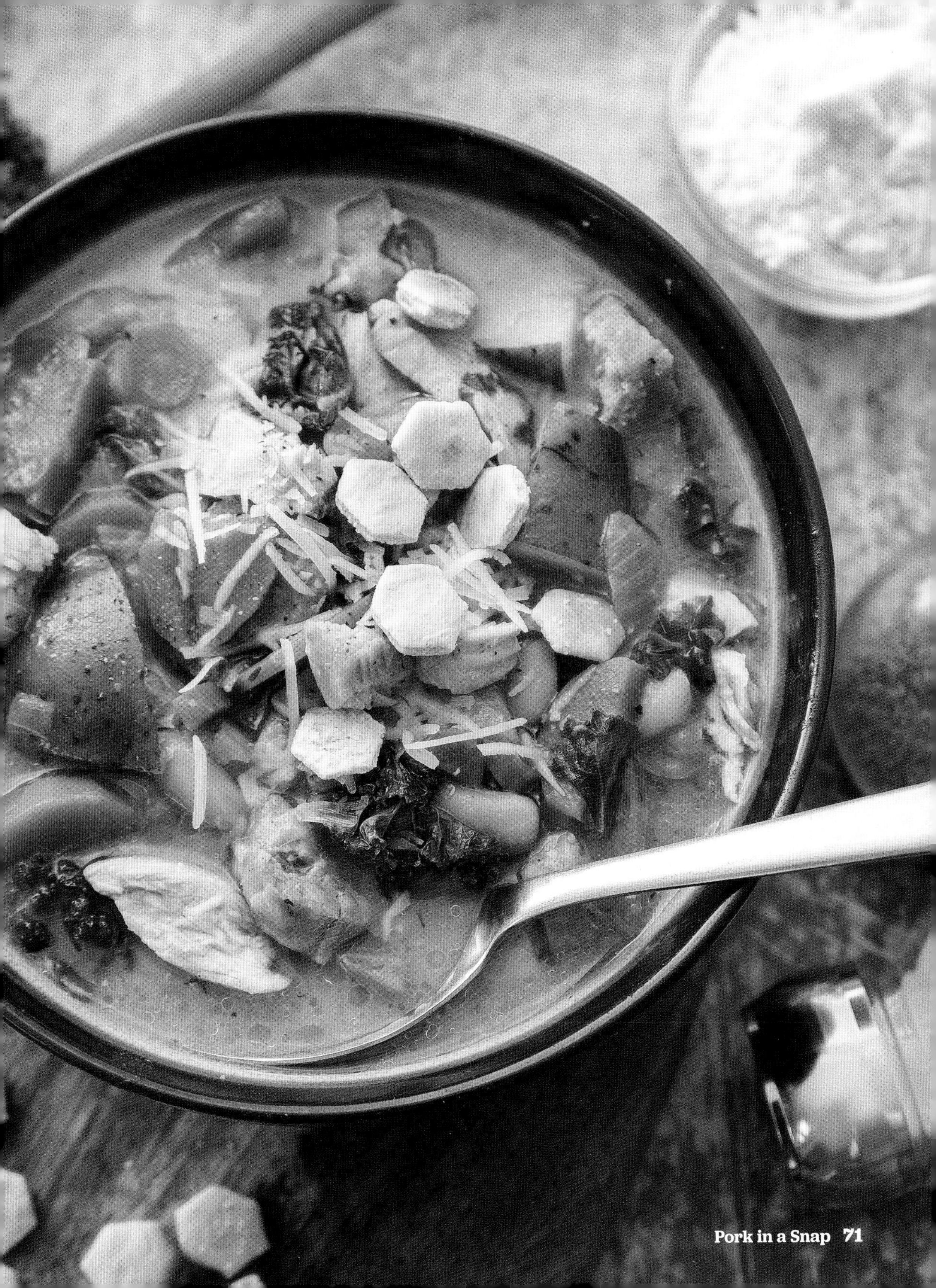

Serves
4

Cajun Jambalaya Packs

Ingredients

» **1 pound raw medium shrimp, peeled and deveined**
» **6 to 8 ounces Andouille pork sausage, thinly sliced**
» **One 14.5-ounce can diced tomatoes with garlic and olive oil**
» **2 teaspoons dried minced onion**
» **4 cups cooked rice**
» **1 green bell pepper, cored and diced**
» **3 to 4 teaspoons Cajun seasoning**
» **1 teaspoon hot sauce**

1. Preheat your grill to medium-high heat.

2. In a big bowl, toss together the shrimp, sausage, tomatoes, dried minced onion, cooked rice, bell pepper, Cajun seasoning, and hot sauce. Divide the mixture among four big pieces of foil spritzed with cooking spray.

3. Wrap the foil around the food to make four tent packs, sealing well.

4. Set the foil packs on the grill grate and cover the grill. Cook 8 to 10 minutes or until shrimp are pink and everything is heated through.

5. Open the packs carefully and enjoy.

Sprouts, Pancetta, 'Shrooms & Eggs

Ingredients

- » **1½ pounds Brussels sprouts, thinly sliced**
- » **2 leeks, halved lengthwise and thinly sliced**
- » **1½ tablespoons olive oil, divided**
- » **Salt and black pepper to taste**
- » **4 ounces mushrooms, thinly sliced**
- » **2 garlic cloves, very thinly sliced**
- » **6 ounces pancetta or Canadian bacon, chopped**
- » **8 eggs**
- » **¼ teaspoon crushed red pepper flakes**
- » **2 ounces crumbled feta cheese**
- » **Chives for garnish**

1. Preheat the oven to 400°F and grease or line your sheet pan. Add the Brussels sprouts and leeks to the prepared pan. Drizzle them with 1 tablespoon of the oil and sprinkle with salt and black pepper; toss to coat. Arrange the mushrooms, garlic, and pancetta evenly over the top, drizzle with the remaining oil, and bake about 10 minutes or until the sprouts are crisp-tender.

2. Remove the pan from the oven and create eight wells in the food. Crack one egg into each well and sprinkle the eggs with pepper flakes, salt, and black pepper. Crumble the cheese over everything. Bake 10 minutes more or until the egg whites are set.

3. Garnish as desired.

Serves 4

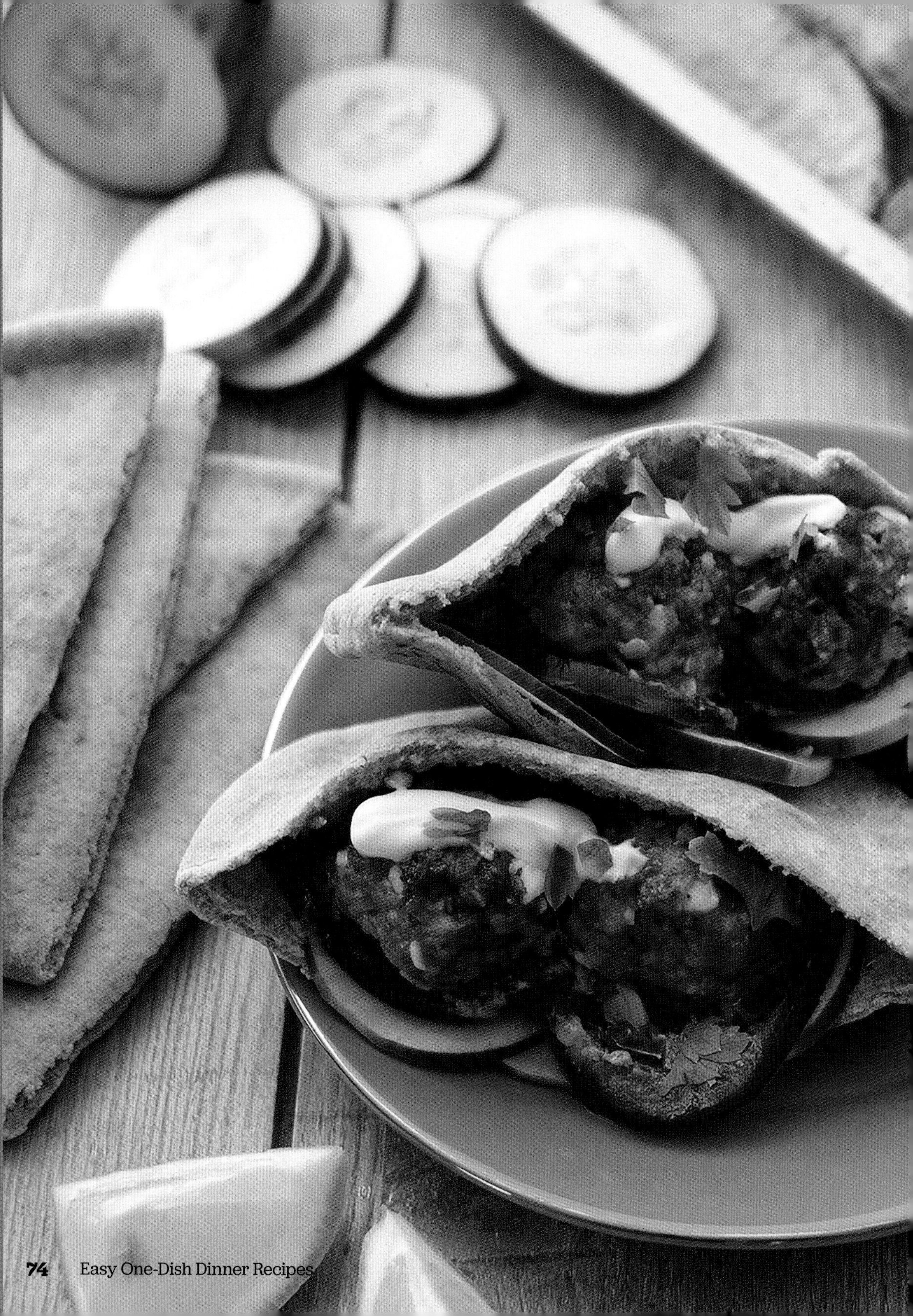

No-Trouble Beef

Everyone knows ground beef is a quick-meal must, but even steaks and roasts can be a part of your easygoing weeknight routines. The following meals range from everyday handhelds to fancier dishes, but they're all destined to become favorite go-to dinners.

Serves
4

Smoky Beef Nachos

Ingredients

- » **1 pound extra-lean ground beef**
- » **2 teaspoons garlic powder**
- » **1½ teaspoons ground cumin**
- » **1 teaspoon chipotle powder**
- » **½ teaspoon salt**
- » **1½ teaspoons cornstarch, divided**
- » **¼ cup water**

- » **8 ounces multigrain tortilla chips**
- » **1 cup salsa con queso**
- » **1½ cup diced tomatoes**
- » **½ cup sliced green onions**
- » **1 or 2 jalapeño peppers, thinly sliced**
- » **Cilantro, sliced radishes, lime wedges, and sour cream for serving**

1. Preheat the oven to 450°F and line your sheet pan with foil. Crumble the beef onto the foil and sprinkle it with the garlic powder, cumin, chipotle powder, salt, and ½ teaspoon of the cornstarch; mix to combine. Drizzle with the water and wrap the excess foil around the meat, sealing tightly. Bake for 20 minutes.

2. Open the foil packet carefully and stir. If the meat is still pink, return it to the oven for a few minutes with the packet open. Once done, remove the packet from the pan, drain the liquid, and set the meat aside.

3. Preheat your oven's broiler with the rack in the top position and carefully line the hot pan with foil.

4. Arrange the chips on the prepared pan. Crumble the drained beef evenly over the chips and drizzle with the salsa con queso. Top evenly with the tomatoes, green onions, and jalapeños and broil for a couple minutes until hot.

5. Sprinkle with cilantro and radishes and squeeze the juice from the lime wedges over the top. Serve with sour cream.

BBQ Meatloaf Meal

Ingredients

- » 1 to 1½ pounds sweet potatoes
- » One 12-ounce package frozen broccoli cuts (don't thaw)
- » ¼ cup olive oil
- » 1 teaspoon seasoned salt
- » Salt and black pepper
- » 1 pound lean ground beef

- » 2 eggs
- » ¼ cup panko breadcrumbs
- » ¾ teaspoon smoked paprika
- » ¾ teaspoon garlic powder
- » ½ cup BBQ sauce, divided
- » Green onions for garnish

1. Preheat the oven to 400°F and grease or line your sheet pan. Cut the sweet potatoes into ½" cubes and arrange them on one end of the pan; arrange the broccoli on the other end. Drizzle the oil evenly over the vegetables. Sprinkle the seasoned salt over the sweet potatoes and the salt and black pepper to taste over the broccoli. Toss to coat, keeping the vegetables separate. Bake for 15 minutes.

2. Meanwhile, in a bowl, combine the ground beef, eggs, breadcrumbs, smoked paprika, garlic powder, 1 teaspoon of salt, and 2 tablespoons of the BBQ sauce. Mix with your hands until combined. Divide the mixture into four thick, oval patties, smoothing the edges. Arrange the patties in the center of the pan, leaving space between them.

3. Spread 1½ tablespoons of the remaining BBQ sauce over each of the patties and bake for 20 minutes or until the meat is done (160°F) and the vegetables are tender.

4. Garnish as desired.

Serves
4-6

Quick Pickle Pot Roast

Ingredients

- » 1 yellow onion, cut into 8 wedges
- » ¾ pound tiny multicolored potatoes, cut in half
- » ½ pound carrot sticks
- » 2 tablespoons olive oil
- » One 1.1-ounce package dry ranch dressing mix
- » One 0.8-ounce package dry brown gravy mix
- » 1¼ pound top sirloin steak
- » 4 whole dill pickles
- » ¼ cup pickle brine

1. Preheat the oven to 425°F and grease or line your sheet pan. Place onion and potatoes on the prepared pan along with carrot sticks. Drizzle with olive oil, toss to coat, and bake for 20 minutes.

2. Stir together the ranch dressing mix and the brown gravy mix and rub the mixture over all sides of the sirloin steak (sprinkle the remaining dry mix over the vegetables if you'd like). Move the vegetables to the outside edges of the pan and set the steak in the center. Lay the dill pickles around the steak and drizzle the food with the pickle brine. Bake for 18 minutes.

3. Remove the pan from the oven and heat the broiler. Broil the food for several minutes, until the steak is nearly done to your liking. Remove the pan from the broiler, tent it with foil, and let it stand for 10 minutes.

4. Slice the steak and pickles and serve.

Gyro Meatball Pitas with Citrus Potatoes

Ingredients

- » 2 ½ pounds russet baking potatoes
- » 1 lemon
- » 1 ½ cups chicken stock
- » ½ cup plus 1 tablespoon olive oil, divided
- » 7 garlic cloves, minced, divided
- » 1 tablespoon plus 1 teaspoon dried oregano, divided
- » 1 ½ teaspoon sea salt, divided
- » ½ pound lean ground beef
- » ½ pound ground lamb or pork
- » ½ cup panko breadcrumbs
- » 2 tablespoons chopped fresh parsley
- » 3 tablespoons grated onion
- » 1 egg
- » ½ teaspoon ground coriander
- » ½ teaspoon ground cumin
- » ½ teaspoon black pepper
- » 2 ounces crumbled feta cheese
- » 8 pita breads
- » Sliced cucumber, sliced tomato, plain Greek yogurt, and lemon wedges for serving

1. Preheat the oven to 400°F and grease or line your sheet pan. Cut the potatoes into ½" thick wedges and arrange them on the prepared pan. Zest and juice the lemon. Measure ⅓ cup of the juice into a medium bowl; set the zest aside. Add the stock, ½ cup of the oil, about two-thirds of the minced garlic, 1 tablespoon of the oregano, and 1 teaspoon of the sea salt to the bowl; stir to combine, pour over the potatoes, and toss to coat. Bake for 20 minutes. Flip the potatoes and bake 30 to 45 minutes longer or until much of the liquid is absorbed.

2. Meanwhile, in a big bowl, combine both types of meat, breadcrumbs, parsley, onion, set-aside lemon zest, egg, coriander, cumin, black pepper, cheese, the remaining garlic, and the remaining ½ teaspoon of sea salt. Blend gently with your hands until just mixed; divide into 20 equal-sized meatballs and set them aside.

3. Discard the juices from the pan, wipe the pan dry, and drizzle the potatoes with the remaining 1 tablespoon of oil. Move the potatoes to one side of the pan and place the meatballs on the other side. Bake an additional 15 to 20 minutes, until the meatballs are done (160°F).

4. Warm the pita bread to soften it, then fill each with cucumber, tomato, meatballs, and yogurt. Serve the potatoes alongside the filled pitas and squeeze juice from the lemon wedges over the top.

Serves 4

Blue Cheese Steak & Celery Bites with Grapes

Serves 4

Ingredients

- » **6 to 8 celery ribs**
- » **1 pint cherry tomatoes**
- » **1 large bunch seedless red grapes**
- » **¼ cup olive oil**
- » **Salt and black pepper to taste**
- » **Four 6- to 8-ounce boneless ribeye or New York strip steaks**
- » **Honey**
- » **Walnut-Blue Cheese Crumbles, recipe on facing page 81**
- » **Blue Cheese Butter, recipe below**

1. Preheat the broiler and grease or line your sheet pan. Prepare the Walnut-Blue Cheese Crumbles and Blue Cheese Butter and set aside.

2. Cut each celery rib into 1" to 2" lengths and dump them onto the prepared pan. Add the tomatoes and grapes beside the celery and drizzle everything with the oil and toss to coat, keeping everything separate. Arrange the celery pieces in a single layer at the edge of the pan, hollow side up. Sprinkle the tomatoes with a little salt and black pepper. Move the tomatoes and grapes to the outside edge of the pan.

3. Season both sides of the steaks with salt and black pepper and arrange them in the center of the pan. Broil a few minutes on each side, until done to your liking, flipping once. If the grapes brown too quickly, remove them from the pan or lower the rack a bit.

4. Stuff the set-aside Walnut-Blue Cheese Crumbles into the hollows of the celery; drizzle them with honey. Put pats of Blue Cheese Butter on the steaks, letting them melt into the meat.

Blue Cheese Butter

In a small bowl, stir together 3 tablespoons of softened butter, 1½ tablespoons of crumbled blue cheese, and ½ teaspoon of chopped fresh thyme.

Walnut-Blue Cheese Crumbles

In a small bowl, stir together 5 ounces of crumbled blue cheese, ¼ cup finely chopped walnuts, ¼ cup chopped fresh parsley, and a bit of black pepper.

Chili Mac

Serves
6

Ingredients

» **1 pound lean ground beef**
» **½ red onion, chopped**
» **1 teaspoon minced garlic**
» **Salt and black pepper to taste**
» **One 15-ounce can petite diced tomatoes**
» **One 6-ounce can tomato paste**
» **One 15-ounce can black beans, drained and rinsed**
» **4 cups beef broth**
» **1 tablespoon chili powder**
» **2 teaspoons ground cumin**
» **1 teaspoon each paprika and dried cilantro**
» **½ teaspoon dried oregano**
» **2 cups uncooked pasta**
» **2 cups shredded sharp cheddar cheese, plus more for serving**
» **Corn chips, for serving**

1. Cook ground beef, onion, and garlic in a big saucepan over medium-high heat until the beef is no longer pink, breaking it apart while it cooks; drain and return it to the pan. Season with salt and black pepper.

2. Add the tomatoes, tomato paste, black beans, broth, chili powder, cumin, paprika, cilantro, and oregano to the saucepan. Bring the mixture to a boil and then stir in the pasta. Cook for 5 to 7 minutes or until the pasta is just al dente, stirring once.

3. Add the cheddar cheese, stirring until melted; remove from the heat, cover, and let stand for 10 minutes.

4. Top with the corn chips and more cheese.

Steak & Mushrooms

Ingredients

» **4 tablespoons butter, divided**
» **4 tender boneless steaks (like sirloin or ribeye)**
» **8 ounces sliced fresh mushrooms**
» **½ cup heavy cream**
» **Sea salt and black pepper to taste**

1. Melt 2 tablespoons of the butter and brush it over both sides of the steaks. Heat a big skillet over medium-high heat and add the steaks. Cook on one side for 3 to 5 minutes (longer for thick steaks). Flip and cook 3 to 5 minutes more or until desired doneness. Transfer to a plate and cover with foil.

2. Wipe out the skillet, set it over medium heat, and add the other 2 tablespoons of butter. When melted, stir in the mushrooms; cook until golden brown and softened. Stir in the heavy cream and simmer on medium-low heat until thickened.

3. Season mushrooms with sea salt and black pepper and serve over the steaks.

Serves 4

Steak & Veggie Skillet

Ingredients

» **1 pound boneless New York strip steak, patted dry**
» **Salt and black pepper**
» **⅓ cup Dijon mustard**
» **1 tablespoon red wine vinegar**
» **1 teaspoon honey**
» **Pinch of cayenne pepper**
» **1 tablespoon water**
» **2½ teaspoons minced garlic, divided**
» **Olive oil**
» **1 bunch green onions, thinly sliced, divided**
» **One 10-ounce package frozen peas**
» **1 pound asparagus, trimmed and cut into 1" pieces**

1. Season both sides of the steak with salt and black pepper. Whisk together the mustard, vinegar, honey, cayenne, water, ½ teaspoon of the garlic, 2½ tablespoons of the oil, and a little salt and black pepper. Heat a medium cast-iron skillet over medium-high heat. Brush 1 tablespoon of the oil over all the sides of the steak; add to the hot pan. Cook until browned and 5°F below your desired level of doneness (for medium, remove at 140°F), turning occasionally. Transfer the steak to a plate and tent it with foil.

2. Wipe out the skillet, set over low heat, and add 2 tablespoons of oil. Set aside some of the green onions for serving and add the remainder to the skillet along with the remaining 2 teaspoons of garlic. Cook 1 minute, stirring constantly. Add the peas and cook just until thawed, stirring occasionally. Add the asparagus, sprinkle with salt and black pepper, and cook until the asparagus is just tender, about 5 minutes, stirring often. Remove from the heat.

3. Slice the set-aside steak and arrange over the vegetables. Drizzle some of the mustard sauce over the steak and top with the set-aside green onions. Serve the remaining mustard sauce on the side.

Speedy Beef Stir-Fry

Serves
6

Ingredients

» **1 pound sirloin steak**
» **Vegetable oil**
» **One 14-ounce package frozen stir-fry vegetables, thawed**
» **1 teaspoon minced garlic**
» **2 tablespoons soy sauce**
» **Two 3-ounce packages beef ramen noodles**

1. Cut the steak into thin 2"-long strips. Heat a little oil in a big skillet over medium-high heat and add the beef strips. Cook until browned on both sides, turning once.

2. Move the beef toward the edge of the skillet and add the vegetables and garlic to the center; cook for 2 to 3 minutes, stirring the vegetables constantly. Stir the beef into the vegetables and add the soy sauce; cook 2 minutes longer or until the vegetables are tender.

3. Meanwhile, cook the noodles according to the package directions, adding the seasoning packets if you'd like; drain. Serve the meat and vegetables over the noodles.

Monterey Meatloaf

Ingredients

- » **1 pound ground beef**
- » **1½ cups medium salsa**
- » **¼ cup grated Parmesan cheese**
- » **¼ cup shredded Monterey Jack cheese**
- » **1 egg**
- » **1 cup crushed saltine crackers**

1. Melt 2 tablespoons of the butter and brush it over both sides of the steaks. Heat a big skillet over medium-high heat and add the steaks. Cook on one side for 3 to 5 minutes (longer for thick steaks). Flip and cook 3 to 5 minutes more or until desired doneness. Transfer to a plate and cover with foil.

2. Wipe out the skillet, set it over medium heat, and add the other 2 tablespoons of butter. When melted, stir in the mushrooms; cook until golden brown and softened. Stir in the heavy cream and simmer on medium-low heat until thickened.

3. Season mushrooms with sea salt and black pepper and serve over the steaks.

Serves 4-6

Pineapple Beef Stir-Fry

Serves 4-6

Ingredients

- » **One 6-ounce can pineapple juice**
- » **2 tablespoons chicken broth**
- » **1 tablespoon brown sugar**
- » **1 tablespoon soy sauce**
- » **⅛ teaspoon cayenne pepper**
- » **½ pound top sirloin steak, cut into thin bite-size strips**
- » **1 tablespoon cornstarch**
- » **¾ teaspoon olive oil, divided**
- » **Salt to taste**
- » **1 carrot, thinly sliced on the diagonal**
- » **½ small onion, chopped**
- » **1 small green bell pepper, thinly sliced**
- » **½ cup sugar snap peas**
- » **½ cup sliced fresh mushrooms**
- » **⅓ cup unsweetened pineapple tidbits**
- » **Sesame seeds**

1. For the marinade, in a small bowl, whisk together the pineapple juice, broth, brown sugar, soy sauce, and cayenne pepper; transfer ⅓ cup to a big zippered plastic bag and chill the remainder. Add the steak to the bag, zip it closed, and turn to coat the steak; chill for about an hour.

2. Drain and discard the marinade from the bag. In a small bowl, whisk together the cornstarch and reserved marinade until smooth; set aside. In a big skillet, fry the steak in ½ teaspoon of hot oil for several minutes, until no longer pink. Transfer the steak to a plate, season with salt, and cover with foil.

3. Sauté the carrot and onion for 4 minutes. Add the remaining ¼ teaspoon of oil with the bell pepper, snap peas, and mushrooms and sauté 3 to 4 minutes more, until crisp-tender. Whisk the cornstarch mixture again and add it to the skillet; bring to a boil, stirring constantly for 2 minutes or until thickened. Stir in the pineapple and the set-aside steak to heat through. Sprinkle with the sesame seeds.

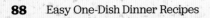

If you don't feel like grilling, try baking your burgers in the oven or cooking them on a pan or griddle instead!

Makes
6

Teriyaki Onion Burgers

Ingredients

- » **1½ pounds lean ground beef**
- » **½ cup teriyaki sauce, divided**
- » **One 3-ounce can French fried onions, crushed**
- » **6 hamburger buns, split**
- » **2 cups green cabbage, finely shredded**

1. Grease your grill grate and preheat the grill to high heat. Mix the ground beef, ¼ cup plus 2 tablespoons of the teriyaki sauce, and the French fried onions; shape into six patties.

2. Grill the patties for 5 minutes on each side or until done to your liking, brushing occasionally with the remaining 2 tablespoons of teriyaki sauce. Spritz the cut sides of the buns with cooking spray and grill them until toasted. Serve the burgers and cabbage on the toasted buns.

Coffee Coriander Cheeseburgers

Ingredients

- » **1 tablespoon fresh ground coffee**
- » **2 teaspoons brown sugar**
- » **2 teaspoons coarse black pepper**
- » **½ teaspoon ground coriander**
- » **½ teaspoon dried oregano**
- » **½ teaspoon sea salt**
- » **2 pounds lean ground beef**
- » **Brewed coffee**
- » **Sliced provolone cheese**
- » **Buns and favorite toppings, for serving**

1. Grease the grill grates and preheat your grill to medium-high heat.

2. Mix the ground coffee, brown sugar, coarse black pepper, ground coriander, dried oregano, and sea salt. Form the ground beef into eight ½" thick patties. Make a slight indentation in the center of each. Sprinkle about 1 teaspoon of the coffee mixture over each patty, pressing to adhere. Set on the hot grill rack and cook for 4 minutes; flip, brush with brewed coffee, and cook until done to your liking. Immediately put a slice of provolone cheese on each patty and set on the buns.

3. Add your favorite toppings and enjoy.

Serves
8

Cuban Meatballs

Serves 4

Ingredients

- » **1 tablespoon olive oil**
- » **1 cup chopped frozen onion**
- » **2 teaspoons minced garlic**
- » **¼ cup chopped pimento-stuffed olives**
- » **¼ cup chopped raisins**
- » **1 teaspoon ground cumin**
- » **¼ teaspoon each salt and black pepper**
- » **¾ pound ground beef**
- » **½ pound ground pork**
- » **One 14-ounce can tomato sauce**
- » **¼ teaspoon ground allspice**
- » **1 tablespoon red wine vinegar**

1. Preheat your broiler. Meanwhile, heat the oil in a big skillet on medium-high heat. Add the onion and cook until thawed. Stir in the garlic and cook 1 minute longer.

2. In a big bowl, stir together the olives, raisins, cumin, salt, black pepper, and half of the onion mixture. Add the beef and pork and mix until just combined. Form into 1½" balls and arrange them on a foil-lined broiler pan. Broil until cooked through, 10 to 12 minutes.

3. Add the tomato sauce and allspice to the onion mixture remaining in the skillet and bring to a boil over medium heat. Remove from the heat and stir in the vinegar. Place the meatballs in the sauce and stir gently.

Reuben Crescents

Ingredients

» **One 12-ounce package refrigerated big and flaky crescent rolls**

» **¼ cup Thousand Island dressing**

» **6 ounces sliced deli corned beef**

» **6 ounces sliced Swiss cheese**

» **1 cup sauerkraut, well drained and squeezed dry**

» **¼ cup horseradish mustard**

» **1 teaspoon crushed caraway seeds**

1. Preheat your oven to 375°F. While the oven is heating, separate the crescent roll dough into four rectangles. Arrange two of the rectangles on an ungreased cookie sheet, short ends together; press to 5" x 14". Press the center seam and perforations between the rolls to seal them well. Spread the Thousand Island dressing over the rectangle to within ¼" of the edge. Top with the corned beef, Swiss cheese, and sauerkraut.

2. Press the remaining rectangles together in the same way and spread with the horseradish mustard; position mustard side down on top of the sauerkraut. Brush the top with a little water and sprinkle with the crushed caraway seeds. Bake for 20 minutes, until deep golden brown.

3. Slice and serve warm.

Serves
6

Serves
6

Sloppy Joes & Seasoned Fries

Ingredients

- » **1¼ pounds lean ground beef**
- » **½ cup diced onion**
- » **One 10.75-ounce can fiesta nacho cheese soup**
- » **⅓ cup ketchup**
- » **Buns, for serving**

- » **1 package frozen French fries**
- » **Cooking spray**
- » **Seasoning of choice (we recommend rosemary and garlic, paprika and cayenne pepper, or Parmesan cheese and coarse black pepper)**

1. For the sloppy joes, in a big skillet over medium-high heat, cook the ground beef and onion together until the meat is brown and the onion is tender, crumbling the meat as it cooks; drain. Stir in the fiesta nacho cheese soup and ketchup. Cover and cook on low for 15 minutes, until heated through, stirring occasionally. Serve on buns.

2. For the fries, prepare the frozen French fries according to the package directions. Immediately spritz them with cooking spray and sprinkle with your favorite seasonings.

Shepherd's Pie

Ingredients

- » **3 medium white potatoes**
- » **¼ cup softened butter**
- » **¼ cup milk**
- » **¾ cup shredded sharp cheddar cheese, divided**
- » **1½ teaspoons salt, divided**
- » **1 tablespoon vegetable oil**
- » **½ pound ground beef**
- » **½ cup chopped onion**
- » **1 teaspoon minced garlic**
- » **¾ cup tomato sauce**
- » **2 cups frozen peas and carrots combo**
- » **½ cup Guinness beer or water**
- » **1 tablespoon steak sauce**
- » **1 teaspoon dried thyme**
- » **½ cup beef broth**

1. In an 8" or 9" oven-safe skillet, cook the potatoes in boiling water until tender but not mushy; drain well, transfer to a bowl, and mash. Stir in the butter, milk, ½ cup cheddar, and 1 teaspoon salt; set aside and wipe out the skillet.

2. Heat the oil in the same skillet over medium heat; add the ground beef, onion, and garlic and cook until the meat is done, crumbling while it cooks. Drain off the grease and return the meat to the skillet. Add the tomato sauce and veggie combo and cook 4 to 5 minutes, stirring often. Pour in the beer and steak sauce; stir in the thyme and the remaining ½ teaspoon of salt.

3. Bring to a boil, reduce the heat, and simmer 10 minutes or until the liquid thickens and has reduced by about half. Add the broth and bring to a boil again; reduce the heat and simmer 20 to 25 minutes, until thick and glossy, stirring occasionally. Remove the skillet from the heat.

4. Preheat your oven to 350°F. Spread the set-aside mashed potato mixture evenly over the top of the food in the skillet and sprinkle with the remaining ¼ cup of cheddar. Bake 30 to 45 minutes, until everything is heated through and the potatoes just start to brown.

Serves 4-6

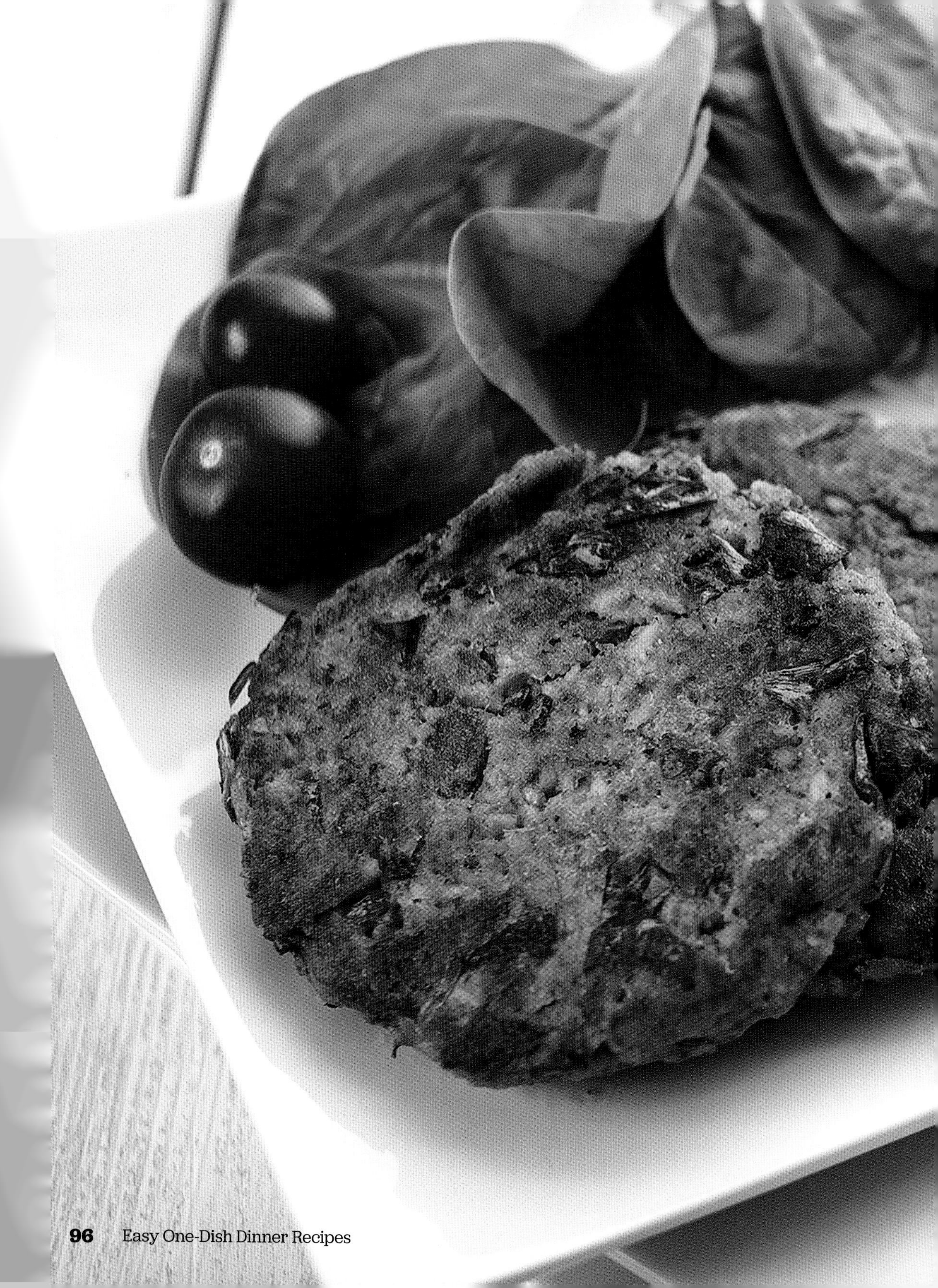

Effortless Seafood

Seafood elevates any meal—calling to mind our favorite special nights out at high-end restaurants or vacation hot spots. Use these recipes to make seafood easy, manageable, and approachable (and just as delicious) when you're cooking in your own kitchen!

Chipotle-Lime Shrimp Bake

Ingredients

» 1½ pounds tiny red potatoes, halved

» 1 tablespoon olive oil

» ¾ teaspoon sea salt, divided

» 3 limes, halved

» ¼ cup unsalted butter, melted

» 1 teaspoon ground chipotle pepper

» ½ pound fresh asparagus

» ½ pound broccoli or broccolini, broken into florets

» 1 pound uncooked shrimp, peeled and deveined

» Cilantro for garnish

1. Preheat the oven to 400°F and grease or line your sheet pan. Toss the potatoes onto the prepared pan; drizzle with the oil, sprinkle with ¼ teaspoon of the sea salt, and toss to coat. Arrange in a single layer and bake for 30 minutes.

2. Meanwhile, squeeze ⅓ cup of juice from the limes; reserve the remaining fruit and the shells that have been squeezed. To the juice, add the butter, chipotle pepper, and the remaining ½ teaspoon sea salt.

3. Remove the pan from the oven and stir the potatoes. Arrange the asparagus, broccoli, shrimp, and all the reserved limes on top of the potatoes and pour the set-aside lime juice mixture evenly over everything. Bake 15 minutes or until the shrimp turn pink and the vegetables are tender.

4. Garnish as desired.

"Everything" Smoked Salmon Egg Bake

Ingredients

- » Coconut oil
- » 16 eggs
- » ½ cup plus 2 tablespoons milk
- » 2 tablespoons chopped fresh dill
- » 1 teaspoon salt
- » ¼ teaspoon black pepper
- » 1 heaping cup halved grape tomatoes
- » 2 tablespoons capers
- » 4 ounces smoked salmon, chopped

- » ½ red onion, thinly sliced
- » 4 ounces cream cheese, cut into small pieces
- » 1 teaspoon poppy seeds
- » ¾ teaspoons dried minced onion
- » ¾ teaspoon dried minced garlic
- » 1 teaspoon black or white sesame seeds
- » 1 teaspoons coarse sea salt

1. Preheat the oven to 300°F and grease your sheet pan generously with coconut oil. In a big bowl, whisk together the eggs, milk, dill, salt, and black pepper and pour the mixture into the prepared pan.

2. Distribute the tomatoes, capers, smoked salmon, red onion, and cream cheese evenly over the eggs. Mix the poppy seeds, dried minced onion, dried minced garlic, sesame seeds, and coarse sea salt and sprinkle evenly over the egg mixture. Bake for 25 minutes or until set.

3. Cut into serving-size pieces.

Serves 8

Garlicky Garden Tilapia

Makes 4

Ingredients

- » ¼ cup unsalted butter, melted
- » 4 garlic cloves, minced
- » 2 tablespoons lemon juice
- » 1 teaspoon Italian seasoning
- » 1 pound fresh asparagus
- » 1½ cups cherry tomatoes
- » ¼ cup olive oil, divided
- » Salt and black pepper to taste
- » Four 6-ounce tilapia fillets, thawed if frozen
- » 2 ciabatta rolls for serving, split
- » Parsley for garnish

1. Preheat the oven to 425°F and grease or line your sheet pan. In a small bowl, whisk together the butter, garlic, lemon juice, and Italian seasoning; set aside 2 tablespoons of the mixture to use for the rolls.

2. Arrange the asparagus and tomatoes in a single layer in the prepared pan; drizzle them with the oil, sprinkle with salt and black pepper, and toss to coat. Move the vegetables to the outside edges of the pan. Arrange the tilapia in the center of the pan and drizzle with the butter mixture. Bake for 10 minutes.

3. Spread the set-aside butter mixture evenly over the cut sides of the rolls; set the rolls on a piece of foil and place it gently on the vegetables. Bake a few minutes more, until the rolls are warm, the fish flakes easily with a fork, and the tomatoes begin to burst.

4. Garnish as desired.

Mediterranean Trout

Ingredients

- One 2-pound trout fillet
- 1 lemon, thinly sliced
- ¼ red onion, thinly sliced
- 1 cup assorted olives
- 1 cup cherry tomatoes, halved
- Several marinated sweet or hot peppers
- 1 tablespoon capers
- 1 zucchini, sliced into half-moons
- 1 yellow summer squash, sliced into half-moons
- ¼ cup olive oil
- Sea salt and coarse black pepper to taste
- Whole peppercorns, optional
- 1 to 2 tablespoons chopped fresh oregano, rosemary, sage, or thyme, plus sprigs for garnish
- 2 tablespoons butter, sliced

1. Preheat the oven to 425°F and grease or line your sheet pan. Set the trout on the prepared pan, tucking the thin end under so it cooks evenly.

2. Arrange the lemon, onion, olives, tomatoes, peppers, capers, zucchini, and yellow squash on and around the trout. Drizzle the oil over everything and sprinkle with the sea salt, black pepper, and chopped herbs. Scatter the butter evenly over the top. Bake for 20 to 30 minutes or until the trout flakes easily with a fork.

3. If you added them, remove the peppercorns before serving. Garnish as desired.

Serves 6

Lingonberry Salmon

Ingredients

- » **4 salmon fillets**
- » **2 zucchini**
- » **2 fennel bulbs**
- » **3 tablepoons olive oil, plus more as needed**
- » **1½ teaspoons fresh thyme leaves**
- » **1 tablespoon lime juice, plus more as needed**
- » **½ pound cherry tomatoes**
- » **Salt and coarse black pepper**
- » **¼ cup lingonberry jam**
- » **1 tablespoon soy sauce**
- » **Cayenne pepper to taste**

1. Preheat the oven to 400°F and grease or line your sheet pan. Lay the salmon fillets down on the center of the pan, skin side down. Cut the zucchini and fennel bulbs in half lengthwise; cut the fennel into thin wedges and arrange the vegetables around the outside of the pan. In a medium bowl, stir together 3 tablespoons of olive oil and the fresh thyme leaves; drizzle evenly over the vegetables and toss to coat.

2. Drizzle a little more olive oil and lime juice over the cherry tomatoes and add them to the empty area of the pan. Sprinkle everything generously with salt and coarse black pepper. Bake 15 to 17 minutes, until the salmon flakes easily and the vegetables are crisp-tender.

3. Meanwhile, stir together the lingonberry jam, soy sauce, lime juice, and cayenne pepper. Remove the food from the oven, but don't turn off the heat.

4. Spoon the jam mixture over the salmon and return to the oven until the sauce bubbles.

Salmon-Dill Pasta

Ingredients

- » **One 1-pound 1" thick salmon fillet**
- » **8 ounces uncooked thin spaghetti noodles**
- » **½ cup dry white wine**
- » **1 finely chopped shallot**
- » **Water**
- » **1 pound asparagus, cut into 1" pieces**
- » **3 tablespoons lemon juice**
- » **4 teaspoons capers**
- » **One 4-ounce jar pimentos, drained**
- » **½ cup sour cream**
- » **1 to 2 teaspoons salt**
- » **⅛ teaspoon cayenne pepper**
- » **¼ teaspoon white pepper**
- » **1 teaspoon lemon pepper**
- » **¼ cups chopped fresh dill**

1. In a big saucepan, combine the salmon fillet, spaghetti noodles, white wine, and shallot. Add enough water to just cover. Bring to a boil, stirring to separate noodles. Reduce heat to a simmer, cover, and cook for 4 minutes.

2. Add the asparagus and cook 3 minutes more, until the asparagus is crisp-tender and the noodles are al dente. Stir in the lemon juice, capers, and pimentos.

3. Remove from the heat and add the sour cream, salt, cayenne pepper, white pepper, lemon pepper, and dill. Stir to combine and break apart the salmon.

Serves 4

Serves 8

Shrimp & Spinach Linguine

Ingredients

- » **16 ounces uncooked linguini noodles, broken in half if desired**
- » **1½ pounds frozen cooked shrimp**
- » **One 14.5-ounce can diced tomatoes**
- » **2 teaspoons minced garlic**
- » **1 tablespoon Italian seasoning**
- » **¼ cup chopped fresh basil**
- » **Juice of 1 lemon**
- » **Salt and black pepper to taste**
- » **4 cups chicken broth**
- » **3 ounces fresh baby spinach**

1. Combine the uncooked noodles, frozen shrimp, tomatoes, garlic, Italian seasoning, basil, lemon juice, salt, and black pepper in a saucepan. Stir in the broth; bring to a boil.

2. Cook over medium heat for 6 minutes, stirring occasionally to separate the noodles. Add the spinach and cook 4 more minutes or until noodles are tender.

Quick Salmon Cakes

Ingredients

- » **10 ounces skinless boneless salmon**
- » **One 14.5-ounce can diced tomatoes with basil, garlic and oregano, drained**
- » **1 cup lightly packed, coarsely chopped fresh spinach**
- » **1 egg**
- » **¾ cup dry Italian breadcrumbs**
- » **Canola oil**

1. Put the salmon into a bowl and flake it with a fork. Mix in the diced tomatoes, spinach, egg, and Italian breadcrumbs. Shape the mixture into six patties, ½" to ¾" thick.

2. Heat a little canola oil in a big skillet over medium heat. Add the patties and cook 4 to 5 minutes or until browned. Turn carefully and cook 4 to 5 minutes more, until heated through.

3. Drain the patties on paper towels before serving.

Serves
6

Garlic Shrimp Tortellini

Serves 8

Ingredients

- » **One 19-ounce package frozen cheese tortellini**
- » **1 head broccoli, cut into small florets**
- » **¼ cup olive oil**
- » **12 ounces shrimp, peeled and deveined, partially thawed if frozen**
- » **2 tablespoons garlic, minced and divided**
- » **¼ cup butter**
- » **½ teaspoon red pepper flakes**
- » **¼ cup flour**
- » **2 cups milk, plus more as needed**
- » **1 cup half-and-half**
- » **4 ounces cream cheese, cubed and softened**
- » **½ cup shredded Parmesan cheese**
- » **Salt and black pepper to taste**

1. Cook the tortellini in a large saucepan according to the package directions, adding the broccoli during the last 3 minutes of cooking time; drain and rinse with cool water and set aside.

2. Heat the now-empty pan over medium-high heat; add the oil, shrimp, and 1 tablespoon of the garlic. Cook until the shrimp turn pink, stirring occasionally. Transfer to a bowl and set aside.

3. Melt the butter in the empty pan over medium heat. Add the red pepper flakes and the remaining 1 tablespoon of garlic; cook about 30 seconds. Whisk in the flour until lightly browned. Gradually whisk in the milk and half-and-half; cook for 6 to 8 minutes or until slightly thickened, whisking constantly. Stir in the cream cheese and Parmesan cheese, stirring until melted, adding a little more milk if the mixture is too thick. Season with salt and black pepper.

4. Add the set-aside tortellini and broccoli and toss to combine. Top each serving with the set-aside shrimp.

Crunchy Fish Tacos

Ingredients

- » **8 frozen battered fish fillets**
- » **Eight 6" corn tortillas**
- » **Vegetable oil**
- » **Shredded green cabbage, black bean and corn salsa, sliced red onion, and sour cream for serving**

1. Bake the fish fillets according to the package directions. Meanwhile, fry the corn tortillas one at a time in a little vegetable oil in a skillet over medium heat until just beginning to brown on one side. Flip over and fold to form a taco shell; fry until golden brown and crispy on both sides.

2. Transfer the fried taco shells to paper towels to drain.

3. Fill the drained shells with baked fish, shredded green cabbage, black bean and corn salsa, and sliced red onion, and drizzle with sour cream.

Shrimp Scampi with Zucchini Noodles

Ingredients

» 1 zucchini

» 2 tablespoons unsalted butter

» 1½ tablespoons olive oil

» 1 tablespoon minced garlic

» ½ to ¾ pounds large shrimp, peeled, deveined and tails removed

» Salt and black pepper to taste

» ¼ cup chicken broth

» Zest and juice from 1 lemon

» ⅛ teaspoon red pepper flakes

» Shredded Parmesan cheese, and chopped tomatoes, for serving

Serves 4-6

1. Cut the zucchini into long strands using a spiral vegetable cutter, then cut the strands to the desired length (or simply cut the zucchini into thin spaghetti-like pieces with a sharp knife). Set aside.

2. In a medium skillet, combine the butter and oil over medium-low heat until melted. Add the garlic and cook for 30 seconds. Add the shrimp, salt, and black pepper and cook 5 minutes or until the shrimp turn pink and opaque, stirring often. Transfer to a plate.

3. Add the broth and lemon juice to the skillet, scraping up any browned bits. Add the set-aside zucchini noodles, lemon zest, and red pepper flakes; stir in the set-aside shrimp. Serve hot topped with Parmesan and tomatoes.

Tuna Noodle Casserole

Serves 4-6

Ingredients

- » **1 cup uncooked egg noodles (we used kluski noodles)**
- » **2 tablespoons butter, divided**
- » **1 shallot, finely chopped**
- » **Salt and black pepper to taste**
- » **1½ tablespoons flour**
- » **¾ cup plus 2 tablespoons chicken broth**
- » **½ cup milk**
- » **½ cup frozen peas**
- » **¼ cup drained and chopped roasted red peppers**
- » **One 5-ounce can tuna packed in water, drained**
- » **½ cup shredded sharp cheddar cheese**
- » **2 tablespoons panko breadcrumbs**
- » **¼ teaspoon dried dill weed**
- » **2 tablespoons Parmesan cheese**

1. Preheat your oven to 375°F. In a 9" or 10" oven-safe skillet, cook the noodles until al dente according to the package directions. Drain the noodles and dump them into a bowl; toss with 1 tablespoon of the butter and set aside.

2. Melt the remaining 1 tablespoon of butter in the same skillet over medium heat. Add the shallot and season with salt and black pepper; sauté 3 to 4 minutes, until the shallot is softened, stirring occasionally. Stir in the flour and heat 30 more seconds.

3. Slowly whisk in the broth, breaking up any lumps. Add the milk and bring the mixture to a boil over medium-high heat. Stir in the peas, reduce the heat to medium, and cook for 5 minutes or until thickened, whisking often.

4. Stir in the roasted peppers and tuna and season again with salt and pepper. Remove the skillet from the heat and stir in the cheddar until it's melted, then stir in the set-aside noodles.

5. Combine the breadcrumbs, dill weed, and Parmesan and sprinkle evenly over the top of the tuna mixture. Spritz the top with a hefty dose of cooking spray and bake uncovered for 20 to 25 minutes or until bubbly and golden brown.

Quick Island Shrimp

Ingredients

- » **One 15-ounce can pineapple chunks**
- » **3 to 4 tablespoons orange marmalade**
- » **½ cup pineapple juice**
- » **½ cup coconut milk**
- » **2 to 3 teaspoons soy sauce**
- » **1 pound large shrimp, peeled and deveined**
- » **Black pepper to taste**

1. Drain the pineapple chunks and set them aside. In a big bowl, stir together the orange marmalade, pineapple juice, coconut milk, and soy sauce.

2. Add the shrimp to the bowl and toss them to coat. Grease the grill grate and preheat your grill to medium-low heat. Push the shrimp and pineapple chunks alternately onto skewers and sprinkle with a healthy shake of black pepper.

3. Grill a few minutes on each side until the shrimp are cooked through and everything has nice grill marks, brushing with the marmalade mixture during cooking.

Garlic Spaghetti

Ingredients

- » ¼ cup olive oil, divided
- » ½ cup panko breadcrumbs
- » 1 tablespoon minced garlic, divided
- » ¼ teaspoon red pepper flakes
- » Salt
- » 1 pound uncooked spaghetti noodles
- » 1 tablespoon butter
- » 3 minced oil-packed anchovy fillets, optional
- » Zest and juice of 1 lemon
- » ⅓ cup grated Parmesan cheese
- » ⅓ cup chopped fresh parsley

1. Heat 3 tablespoons of the oil in a big skillet over medium-high heat. Add the breadcrumbs, 1½ teaspoons of the garlic, and the red pepper flakes. Cook a few minutes until golden. Transfer to paper towels; wipe out the skillet, and set aside.

2. Bring a big pot of salted water to a boil and cook the spaghetti to your desired doneness; drain, reserving 1 cup of the cooking water. Melt the butter in the set-aside skillet and add the remaining 1 tablespoon of oil. Add the anchovies if using and the remaining 1½ teaspoons of garlic; cook about 2 minutes. Lower the heat to medium-low and simmer while the spaghetti cooks.

3. Add the spaghetti to the skillet; toss to coat. Stir in the lemon zest and juice and the Parmesan cheese. Add the reserved cooking water a little at a time to thicken the sauce. Stir in the parsley and ¾ of the breadcrumb mixture. Serve immediately topped with the remaining breadcrumb mixture.

Serves 4

Easy Vegetarian

Changing up your routine for Meatless Mondays can feel daunting, but the recipes in this section make vegetarian cooking quick, easy, and approachable. You'll end up with a delicious, filling meal without a lot of fuss or clean-up. These vegetable-packed powerhouses are sure to become regular family favorites.

Squash & Feta Dinner Salad

Serves 4

Ingredients

- » **1½ pounds acorn squash, halved lengthwise, seeded and cut into ¼" slices**
- » **8 tablespoons olive oil, divided**
- » **1½ teaspoons coarse salt, divided**
- » **¼ teaspoon coarse black pepper**
- » **4 cups cubed ciabatta bread**
- » **½-pound block feta cheese, cut into ½" to 1" cubes**
- » **¼ cup red wine vinegar**
- » **1 teaspoon honey**
- » **1 teaspoon fresh thyme leaves**
- » **6 to 8 cups torn radicchio or endive or two 5-ounce packages mixed greens**
- » **Pumpkin seeds**
- » **Chopped Anaheim peppers**

1. Arrange an oven rack in the top third of the oven and preheat to 400°F. Grease or line your sheet pan.

2. Put the squash on the sheet pan and toss with 2 tablespoons of the oil, the black pepper, and 1 teaspoon of the salt. Arrange in a single layer and bake 15 to 20 minutes, until the squash just begins to brown around the edges; flip the squash over and put the bread and cheese cubes over the top. Bake 15 to 20 minutes longer, until the squash is tender, and the bread is toasted.

3. Meanwhile, whisk together the vinegar, honey, thyme, the remaining 6 tablespoons of olive oil, and the remaining ½ teaspoon of salt; set aside.

4. Remove the pan from the oven and let stand for 5 minutes. Pile the radicchio or greens on the hot food, drizzle with the vinegar mixture, and toss to coat. Scatter the pumpkin seeds and Anaheim peppers on top. Serve immediately.

Rainbow Adobo Portobello Tacos

Ingredients

- » 1½ tablespoons Adobo Seasoning, recipe below
- » ¾ pound portobello mushrooms, sliced
- » ½ to 1 red onion, sliced
- » 1 red bell pepper, cut into strips
- » 1 or 2 large carrots, cut into sticks
- » 1 yellow summer squash, cut into strips
- » 2 tablespoons olive oil
- » Juice of 2 limes
- » Taco shells
- » Romaine lettuce leaves
- » Guacamole, black olives, diced tomatoes, and shredded Colby Jack cheese for serving

Serves 4

1. Preheat the oven to 425°F and grease or line your sheet pan. Prepare the Adobo Seasoning and set aside. Arrange the mushrooms, onion, bell pepper, carrots, and squash on the prepared pan and drizzle with the oil and lime juice. Sprinkle everything evenly with the Adobo Seasoning and bake for 15 minutes, until the vegetables are tender.

2. Fill the taco shells with lettuce, mushrooms, and vegetables. Add guacamole, olives, tomatoes, and cheese.

Adobo Seasoning

Mix 2 tablespoons of salt, 1 tablespoon of paprika, 2 teaspoons of black pepper, 1½ teaspoons each of onion powder, dried oregano, and ground cumin, and 1 teaspoon each of garlic powder and chili powder. Keep in a sealed jar.

Vegetable Chili & Buttermilk Biscuits

Serves 6

Ingredients

- » 3 tablespoons vegetable oil
- » 1 tablespoon chili powder
- » ½ teaspoon ground cumin
- » 1¾ teaspoons salt, divided
- » 1 head cauliflower
- » 1 poblano pepper
- » 4 green onions
- » ¾ cup stone-ground cornmeal
- » ½ cup flour
- » 2 teaspoons baking powder
- » 1 tablespoon brown sugar
- » ¼ cup unsalted butter
- » ⅔ cup buttermilk
- » ⅔ cup shredded sharp cheddar cheese, divided, plus more for serving
- » One 15-ounce can black beans
- » One 8-ounce can tomato sauce
- » 1¼ cups frozen sweet corn (don't thaw)
- » 1½ cups vegetable broth
- » Parsley for garnish

1. Preheat the broiler. In a big bowl, stir together the oil, chili powder, cumin, and ½ teaspoon of salt. Cut the cauliflower into small florets, seed and dice the poblano, and chop the green onions; add the vegetables to the oil mixture and stir to coat. Dump everything onto the prepared sheet pan, arrange in a single layer, and broil for 7 to 10 minutes, until brown around the edges.

2. Meanwhile, whisk together the cornmeal, flour, baking powder, brown sugar, and ¾ teaspoon of salt. Cut the butter into cubes and work into the dry ingredients with your fingers until the mixture is crumbly. Add the buttermilk and ⅓ cup of the cheese, stirring with a fork until combined.

3. To the roasted vegetables, add the beans with their liquid, the tomato sauce, frozen corn, broth, and ½ teaspoon of salt; stir gently. Scoop the biscuit dough on top of the veggie mixture in 12 mounds, leaving space between them. Sprinkle the dough evenly with the remaining ⅓ cup of the cheese. Bake for 25 to 30 minutes, until the chili starts bubbling and the biscuits turn golden brown.

4. Sprinkle with extra cheese and garnish as desired.

Veggie Taco Pizza

Serves 4

Ingredients

- » **One 12" ready-to-bake pizza crust**
- » **One 16-ounce can refried beans**
- » **1 tablespoon canola oil**
- » **One 1-ounce package taco seasoning**
- » **One 15-ounce can black beans, drained and rinsed**
- » **One 2.25-ounce can sliced black olives, drained**
- » **½ cup chopped tomatoes**
- » **½ cup sliced green onions**
- » **½ cup frozen or canned corn kernels**
- » **1 to 2 cups Mexican cheese blend**
- » **Favorite toppings, for serving**

1. Preheat the oven to 425°F. Set the crust on a pizza pan.
2. Stir together the refried beans, oil, and taco seasoning; spread evenly over the crust. Sprinkle the black beans, olives, tomatoes, green onions, corn, and cheese over the top.
3. Bake for 12 minutes or until the cheese is melted.
4. Let everyone top off their serving the way they like it.

Southwest Hash

Ingredients

- » 3 tablespoons olive oil
- » 2 cups diced turnips or potatoes
- » 1½ tablespoons taco seasoning
- » 1 teaspoon salt
- » ½ onion, diced
- » 1 bell pepper, any color, diced
- » 1 teaspoon minced garlic
- » 4 eggs
- » Toppings such as shredded Mexican cheese, salsa, cilantro, or lime wedges

1. Heat the oil in a big skillet over medium-high heat. Add the turnips or potatoes, taco seasoning, and salt and cook for about 5 minutes, stirring occasionally. Add the onion, bell pepper, and garlic and cook 3 more minutes, until the vegetables begin to soften.

2. Make four wells in the hash and crack an egg in each. Cover and cook a few minutes more, until the egg whites are set.

3. Add desired toppings.

Serves 4

Smoky Spinach & Artichoke Pizza

Ingredients

» **1 tablespoon cornmeal**
» **1 cup warm water**
» **One 0.25-ounce package active dry yeast**
» **1 tablespoon sugar**
» **2½ cups flour, plus more for sprinkling**
» **1 teaspoon salt**
» **¼ cup olive oil, divided**
» **1 teaspoon Italian seasoning**
» **6 garlic cloves**
» **1½ cups shredded smoked provolone cheese**
» **One 6-ounce bag fresh baby spinach**
» **Two 6.5-ounce jars marinated artichoke hearts**
» **Red pepper flakes to taste**

1. Preheat the oven to 425°F and sprinkle the cornmeal evenly on your sheet pan.

2. Pour the water into the bowl of a stand mixer and add the yeast and sugar. Let stand for 10 to 15 minutes until the yeast becomes frothy. Add the flour and mix using the hook attachment. Add the salt and 2 tablespoons of the oil. Mix for 3 to 4 minutes, until the dough is firm. Let stand for 3 to 4 minutes.

3. Sprinkle a work surface and a rolling pin with a little flour. Roll the dough into a rectangle a little smaller than the prepared pan and carefully transfer the dough to the pan; stretch the dough to the corners. Spread 1 tablespoon of the remaining oil all over the top of the dough and sprinkle evenly with the Italian seasoning, garlic, and half the cheese.

4. In a bowl, mix the remaining 1 tablespoon of oil with the spinach to coat; arrange the spinach evenly over the cheese. Drain the artichokes and arrange them over the spinach; sprinkle with the remaining cheese and the pepper flakes. Bake for 12 to 15 minutes, until the cheese is bubbly, and the crust is golden brown.

5. Cut into serving-size pieces.

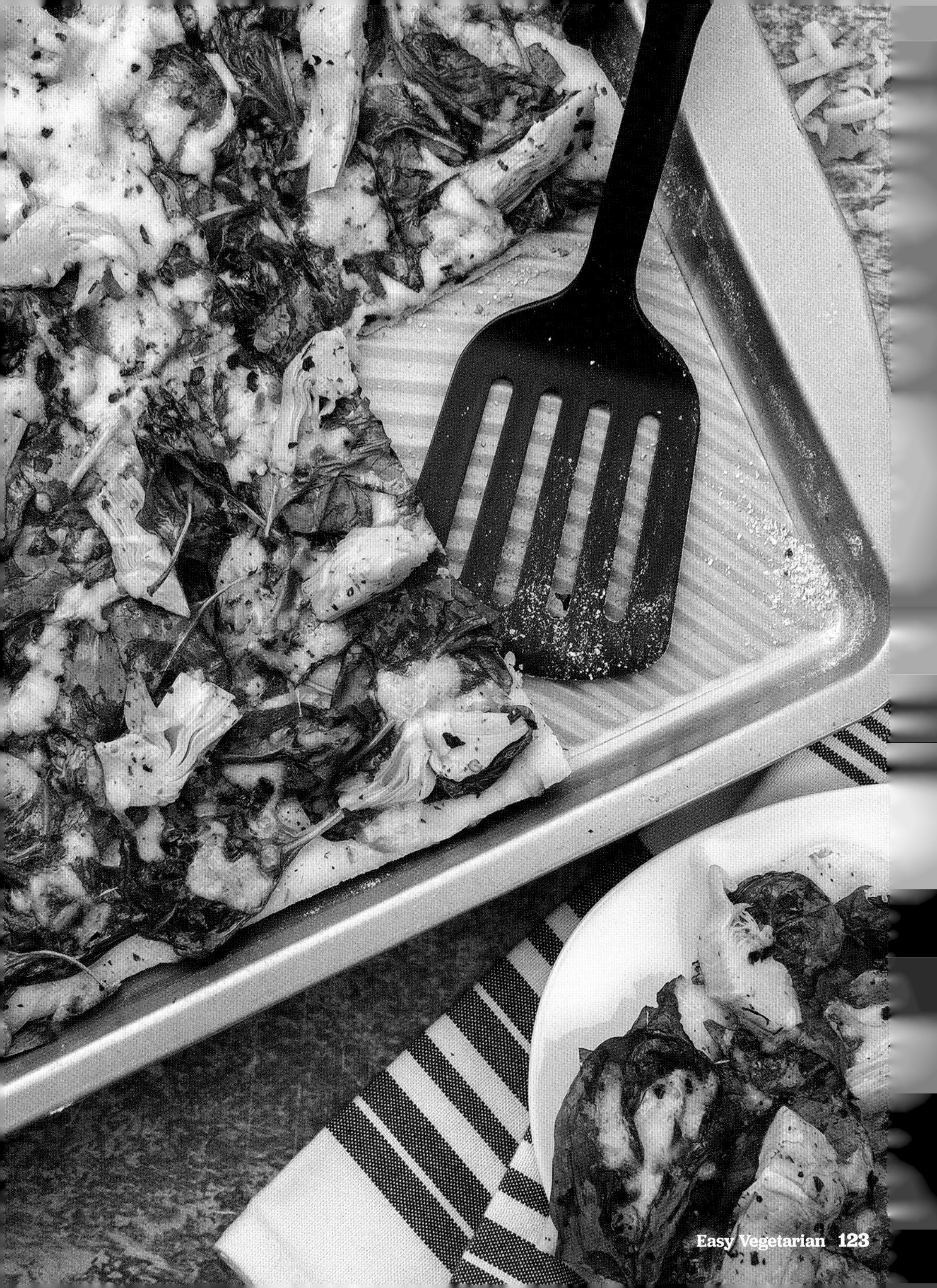

Corn-Stuffed Tomatoes

Ingredients

- » **½ cup corn kernels**
- » **4 medium tomatoes**
- » **½ cup cooked quinoa**
- » **Shredded smoked Gouda**
- » **Shredded farmer cheese**
- » **Seasonings to taste**

1. Dump the corn kernels into a dry skillet over medium-high heat. Cook and stir until nicely charred; set aside. Preheat your broiler.

2. Slice the tops off the tomatoes and carefully scoop out the insides. Put the scooped-out portions in a food processor and pulse until no large chunks remain; drain any excess liquid and dump the processed tomato portion into a bowl with the cooked quinoa and charred corn. Add a small handful each of shredded smoked Gouda and farmer cheese. Stir in your favorite seasonings to taste.

3. Stuff the mixture into the hollowed-out tomatoes, sprinkle with a little more cheese, and set into a muffin pan. Broil 7" to 8" away from the heat for 3 to 5 minutes, until warm, moving the pan closer to the heat during the last minute to brown the tops.

Sweet Potato Chili

Ingredients

- » **2 tablespoons olive oil**
- » **1 large onion, diced**
- » **2 sweet potatoes, peeled and diced**
- » **2 teaspoons garlic, minced**
- » **2 tablespoons chili powder**
- » **1 tablespoon ground cumin**
- » **½ teaspoon chipotle powder**
- » **2 teaspoons salt**
- » **2 ⅔ cups water**
- » **One 15-ounce can black beans, drained and rinsed**
- » **One 15-ounce can crushed tomatoes**
- » **1 tablespoon lime juice**
- » **Sour cream, avocado, and shredded cheese, for serving**

1. Heat the oil in a big skillet over medium-high heat. Add the onion and sweet potatoes and sauté until they are slightly softened, stirring often. Add the garlic, chili powder, cumin, chipotle powder, and salt; heat for 30 seconds, stirring constantly. Add the water and bring to a simmer. Cover, reduce heat to maintain a gentle simmer, and cook for 10 minutes or until the sweet potatoes are tender.

2. Stir in the black beans, tomatoes, and lime juice; heat to simmering, stirring often.

3. Cook to slightly reduce the liquid.

4. Serve with your desired toppings. Omit the cumin and chipotle powder for a less smoky flavor.

Serves
4

Stuffed Portobellos

Ingredients

- » **4 large portobello mushrooms**
- » **1 cup Italian dressing**
- » **One 16-ounce jar roasted red peppers, chopped**
- » **2 cups shredded mozzarella cheese**

> If you don't feel like grilling, try baking your stuffed portobellos in the oven instead!

1. Remove stems and gills from the mushrooms and marinate with the dressing in a zippered plastic bag for at least 1 hour.
2. Drain and grill on the stem side for 5 minutes. Flip over and fill the caps with the red peppers and cheese. Grill until the cheese melts, 5 to 8 minutes more.

Fettuccine Primavera

Ingredients

- » ¼ pound fettuccine noodles
- » 1 tablespoon butter
- » 1½ cups thinly sliced fresh vegetables (we used red bell pepper, carrots, and zucchini)
- » 1½ cups heavy cream
- » ⅓ cup frozen peas, thawed
- » Salt, black pepper, and cayenne pepper to taste
- » 1 cup shredded Italian cheese blend
- » Fresh parsley, chives, and toasted sunflower seeds, for serving

1. In a big skillet, cook the fettuccine noodles according to the package directions; drain, setting aside ½ cup of the cooking liquid.

2. In the same skillet over medium heat, melt the butter. Add the set-aside cooking liquid and the sliced vegetables; cover and cook over medium-low heat for 3 minutes, until the vegetables are just tender. Add the heavy cream, peas, salt, black pepper, and cayenne pepper; bring to a simmer.

3. Toss the set-aside noodles with the vegetables and add the shredded Italian cheese blend; simmer until the cheese melts and the sauce thickens. Serve immediately sprinkled with fresh parsley, chives, and sunflower seeds.

Serves 4

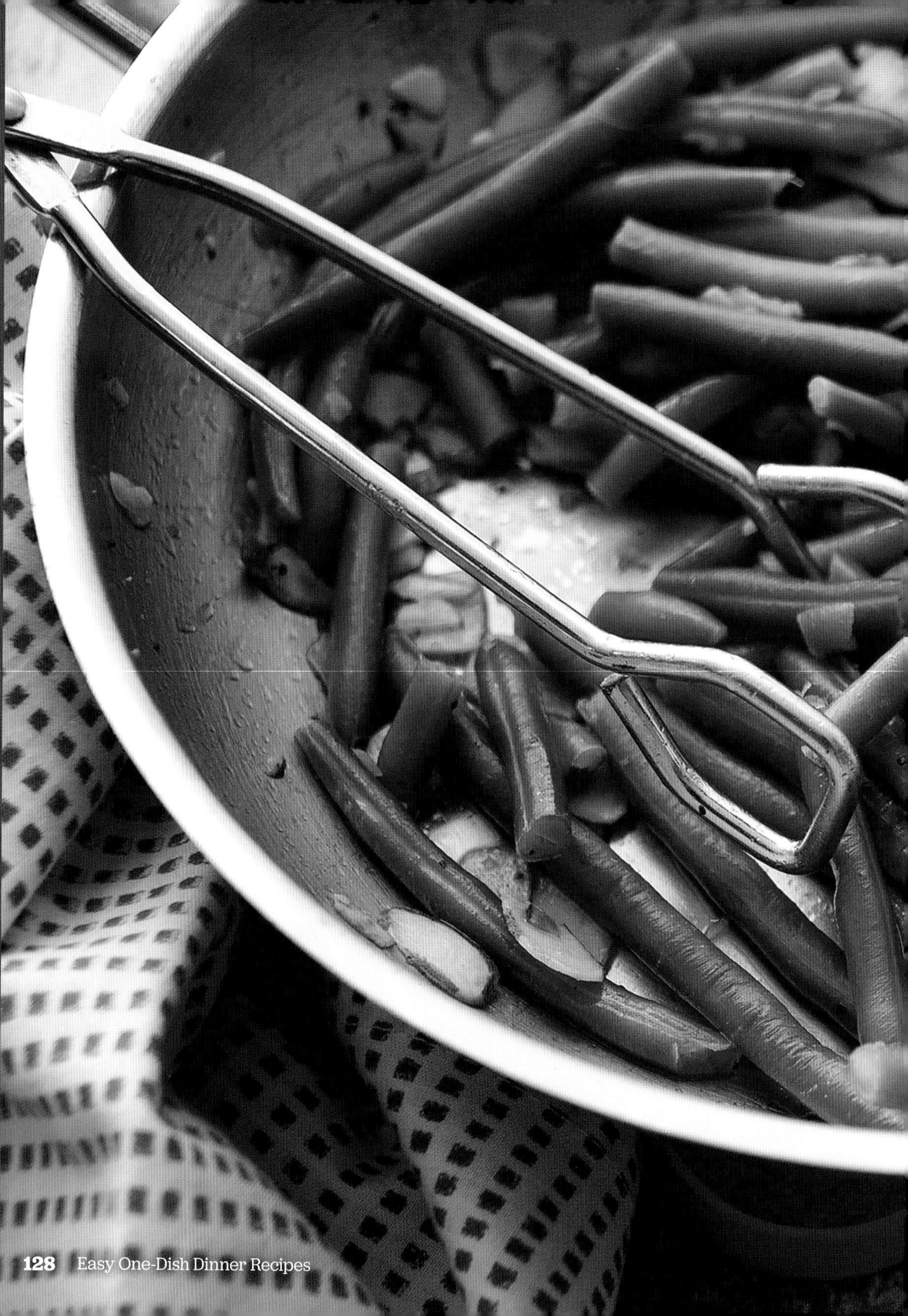

Shortcut Sides

The perfect side can turn any dish into a complete, filling meal. These sides are all quick, easy options for adding some healthy vegetables or filling starches to round out your dinner menu. They're also great dishes to make for potlucks and summer picnics.

Serves
4

Layered Veggie Salad

Ingredients

- » ⅓ cup apple cider vinegar
- » ⅓ cup sugar
- » ¼ cup olive oil
- » 1½ teaspoon salt
- » ¼ teaspoon black pepper
- » ½ red onion, finely chopped
- » 2 celery stalks, finely chopped
- » One 15-ounce can cannellini beans, rinsed and drained

- » 1 cup chopped fresh parsley
- » One 15-ounce can kidney beans, rinsed and drained
- » 1 yellow bell pepper, chopped
- » One 15-ounce can black beans, rinsed and drained
- » 1 tablespoon finely chopped fresh rosemary

1. Whisk together vinegar, sugar, oil, salt, and pepper; divide evenly among eight half-pint fruit jars. In each jar, layer the remaining ingredients. Tighten the lids until serving.

2. To serve, shake the jars to distribute the dressing. Grab a fork and eat right out of the jars. These will keep for several days.

Mashed Sweet Potatoes

Ingredients

» **2 large sweet potatoes**
» **Butter, brown sugar, and cinnamon, for topping**

1. Peel and dice the sweet potatoes.

2. Place in a saucepan with 1" of boiling water and cook uncovered for 10 to 15 minutes or until very tender; drain.

3. Mash well with a fork or potato masher. Add a couple pats of butter and sprinkle with a little brown sugar and cinnamon.

Serves
4

Baked Potatoes Three Ways

Serves
6

Ingredients

» **Russet potatoes**
» **Butter, sour cream, cheese, bacon, or chives, for topping**

Microwave

1. Wash the russet potatoes and poke the skin a few times with a fork.

2. Cook one large potato at a time in the microwave on high power for 4 to 5 minutes; turn and cook 3 to 5 minutes more or until tender. (Shorten the cooking time for small potatoes; for multiple potatoes, increase the cooking time by $2/3$.)

3. Wrap in foil and let stand for 5 minutes before slicing open and adding the toppings.

Pressure Cooker

1. Pour 1 cup of cold water into the cooker and add the trivet/rack.

2. Prick 4 to 8 potatoes with a fork and add them to the cooker, making sure they don't touch the water.

3. Set the cooker to high pressure and cook 10 minutes for small potatoes, 12 minutes for medium potatoes, and 20 minutes for extra-large potatoes.

4. Let the pressure release naturally for 8 to 10 minutes, then open the valve to release the remaining pressure.

5. Slice open and add the toppings.

Oven

1. Wrap pricked potatoes in foil and bake at 350°F for 1 hour or until tender.

2. Slice open and add the toppings.

Cilantro-Lime Rice

Ingredients

- » **1 tablespoon butter**
- » **1 cup long-grain white rice**
- » **Zest of 1 lime**
- » **2 tablespoons lime juice**
- » **½ cup chopped fresh cilantro**

1. In a medium saucepan, boil 2 cups of water; stir in the butter and rice.
2. Cover, reduce heat to low, and simmer for 20 minutes, until tender.
3. Stir in the lime zest, lime juice, and cilantro.

Mexican Corn

Ingredients

- » **One 15-ounce can whole kernel corn, drained**
- » **6 ounces cream cheese, cut into small pieces**
- » **⅓ cup chopped roasted red peppers**
- » **Finely chopped jalapeño pepper to taste**
- » **1 teaspoon garlic salt**

1. In a medium saucepan, combine the corn, cream cheese, roasted red peppers, jalapeño, and garlic salt.
2. Cook over medium heat until warm, stirring constantly to melt the cream cheese.

Serves 4

Zippy Glazed Carrots

Ingredients

- » **4 cups baby carrots**
- » **⅔ cup apple juice**
- » **¼ cup apple jelly**
- » **1 tablespoon Dijon mustard**
- » **Preferred seasonings, for serving**

1. Combine the baby carrots and apple juice in a medium saucepan.

2. Bring to a boil over medium heat; reduce the heat, cover the pan, and simmer 6 to 8 minutes or until the carrots are crisp-tender.

3. Add the apple jelly and Dijon mustard; stir and cook until the carrots are nicely glazed. Season as desired.

Serves 4

Serves
8

Green Beans Almondine

Ingredients

» **1 pound fresh green beans**
» **2 tablespoons butter**
» **¼ cup sliced almonds**
» **2 teaspoons lemon pepper**

1. Steam the green beans until crisp-tender, about 10 minutes (or cook frozen green beans according to the package directions); drain.

2. Meanwhile, melt the butter in a skillet over medium heat. Add the sliced almonds and sauté them until golden; season with the lemon pepper and stir into the green beans.

Roasted Veggies

Ingredients

» **4 to 6 cups cut-up vegetables (such as Brussels sprouts, parsnips, carrots, onions, potatoes, sweet potatoes, or squash)**

» **2 to 3 tablespoons olive oil**

» **Sea salt and coarse black pepper or your favorite seasoning blend to taste**

1. Preheat the oven to 400°F. Line a rimmed baking sheet with foil and spritz the foil with cooking spray.

2. Dump the vegetables onto the prepared pan. Drizzle with the olive oil and sprinkle with sea salt and coarse black pepper or your favorite seasoning blend; toss to coat and arrange the vegetables in a single layer.

3. Bake for 20 to 30 minutes or until fork-tender and nicely browned, turning halfway through baking time (turning creates more even browning but is an optional step).

Parm-Pepper Breadsticks

Ingredients

» **One 11-ounce tube refrigerated breadsticks**
» **Melted butter**
» **6 tablespoons grated Parmesan cheese**
» **¾ teaspoon coarse black pepper**

1. Preheat the oven according to the package directions. Separate the breadsticks and brush them with melted butter.

2. On a plate, mix the Parmesan cheese and coarse black pepper; roll the breadsticks in the mixture and bake according to the package directions.

Makes
12

Serves 8-12

Pesto Cheese Bread

Ingredients

- » **1 Vienna bread loaf**
- » **6 tablespoons melted butter**
- » **3 tablespoons sundried tomato pesto**
- » **Slices of provolone, mozzarella, or fontina cheese**

1. Preheat the oven to 375°F. Line a rimmed baking sheet with foil and spritz the foil with cooking spray.
2. Set the Vienna bread loaf on the foil; cut the loaf into ¾"-thick slices without cutting all the way through the bottom.
3. Stir together the melted butter and sundried tomato pesto and brush the mixture between the bread slices; pour any remainder over the top. Place slices of cheese between each of the cuts.
4. Crimp the foil closely around the bottom half of the loaf and bake for 15 minutes until golden brown.

Index